Local Signs and Wonders

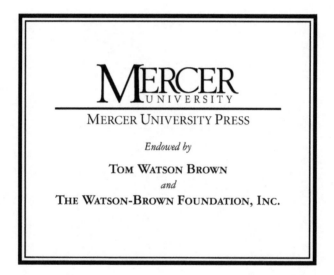

MERCER UNIVERSITY PRESS

Endowed by

TOM WATSON BROWN
and
THE WATSON-BROWN FOUNDATION, INC.

LOCAL SIGNS AND WONDERS

Essays about Belonging to a Place

Richard Rankin

MERCER UNIVERSITY PRESS
MACON, GEORGIA

MUP/ P691

© 2024 by Mercer University Press
Published by Mercer University Press
1501 Mercer University Drive
Macon, Georgia 31207

28 27 26 25 24   5 4 3 2 1

Books published by Mercer University Press are printed on acid-free
paper that meets the requirements of the American National
Standard for Information Sciences—Permanence of Paper for Printed
Library Materials.

Printed and bound in the United States.

This book is set in Adobe Caslon and Georgia (display).

Cover/jacket design by Burt&Burt.

ISBN   978-0-88146-924-0 Print
ISBN   978-0-88146-933-2 eBook
Cataloging-in-Publication Data is available from the Library of
Congress

In Memory of

Mamie Allison Cole

John Odell Haggins

Rozella Hicks Haggins

Ash Spratt

In Honor of

Frank Cree Rankin

Contents

Preface

This collection of essays describes my relationship with our family homestead and, more broadly, with other local people and traditions. The Rankin homeplace is located in a rapidly disappearing rural landscape of the North Carolina Piedmont, in the Stanley Creek watershed, between the old textile-manufacturing towns of Stanley and Mt. Holly. Charlotte, one of the nation's fastest-growing cities, is thirteen miles east. Since my family settled historic Rankintown in the mid-1760s, I am the sixth generation to live here. Before the disappearance of family farming, my ancestors lived in this rural community, practiced agriculture, and gave their name to the place. With local farming largely gone and the Rankintown name almost completely forgotten, I continue to make my home on part of the same family property while working as an independent school headmaster sixteen miles away in Gastonia. Such a long settlement on family land builds a deep affection for and knowledge of the surrounding terrain, local history, and culture. That doesn't mean that the present or the past are accepted uncritically. Part of what it means to live responsibly in a place is to work to solve inequities that occurred or persist and to repair the damage.

A sense of belonging to this place and continuity with its past are unifying themes in all the essays. The surrounding rocks, woods, creeks, and former fields are the natural context. The Native Americans, enslaved people, tenant farmers, ancestors, and neighbors who once lived here form the historical background. My personal identity permeates the locale and grows out of the place's hyper-local history. In my case, the commitment to living in this place comes as part of a multigenerational inheritance. But I believe a newcomer can cultivate a similar attitude and become deeply attached to a place over time. Wanting to belong to a place grows out of a deep yearning to feel at home in the world and then finding a special setting where that feeling is best satisfied.

In an age in which leaving home typically provides better opportunities for employment, new experiences, and a certain kind of freedom, staying put or moving back involves a serious, countercultural commitment. But, I would argue, it also offers a life filled with wonder, beauty, and creativity and leads to unusually strong and deep relationships. The deliberate, thoughtful inhabitant embraces a new kind of artistry, involving a dynamic relationship with the place and its past. Living itself becomes a form of creative expression, one that unifies and enriches the resident, the place, and their shared history within creation. In his attempt to describe the sublime character of such local living, Wendell Berry suggests the concept of marriage—in this case marriage to a place—as the best analogy. In one of his books, Mr. Berry titles the satisfying, healthy relationship that exists between a beloved place and its people as "a continuous harmony."[1]

My relationship with the Rankin homeplace grows out of faith, which for me is a mainline, progressive Protestant Christianity. I believe the Creator unites and sustains everything in an intricate, infinitely complex natural order,

---

[1] Wendell Berry, *A Continuous Harmony: Essays Cultural and Agricultural* (New York: Harcourt, 1972).

full of beauty and bounty. But creation also suffers from human deceit, greed, and predation. In response, belonging to family land necessarily involves stewardship and agency. That means working to protect the natural world and its creatures, repairing them when they are harmed or hurt, and grieving their losses. It also means looking for wildflowers, eating hand-picked blackberries each spring, and experiencing a host of other simple pleasures. Joys and consolations abound when living in a familiar place.

Several other important perspectives inform my writing: a reverence for nature (which I understand as created), a scientific worldview, and advanced historical training. Within these broader categories, the roles of creativity and wonder (which I understand as divine gifts) and an appreciation for wildness are special interests of mine. My sorrow over the disappearance of family farming and the rural landscape and a strong foreboding over environmental threats and damage are evident in several essays. But I hope these losses and fears are partly offset by the spirit of adventure, renewal, and hopefulness that inhabiting my homeplace inspires.

Any serious commitment to a place involves partners. The beautiful character of my homeplace involves a web of relationships with family, friends, and neighbors, some living and more dead. Other strong influences include writers who share a commitment to the importance of their own homeplaces. Like me, many of these people chose to stay put while the world around us changed. With agriculture abandoned as the primary way of life in my area, conservation organizations play a crucial role in preserving family land. In particular, the Catawba Lands Conservancy, our local land trust, provides leadership and expertise.

Stewarding local spaces depends on fellow inhabitants, outside specialists, and supporting environmental organizations and governmental agencies.

These essays were written to honor my homeplace and its residents. In a time of ceaseless change and restlessness, I hope they bear witness to the possibility of living responsibly and well in a familiar place. They convey the deep satisfaction and enjoyment that settledness in a special place affords. And they call us to active stewardship as social and economic forces and environmental degradation imperil the places we love.

1

Willowside at Equipoise

In the late summer of 1938 when Frances Benjamin Johnston came to photograph historic Willowside, the Rankin farm had operated continuously since the mid-1780s, through the rise and fall of slavery, the Civil War, Reconstruction, and the advent of tenant farming. In 1889, the nearby village of Mt. Holly hosted a farmers' encampment and fair that attracted more than 3,000 people from across the state and reflected the preeminence of agriculture. Col. Richard Rankin, who inherited Willowside from his father, took a leading role in the gathering. For more than 170 years, Willowside was a prime example of the thousands of working farms that blanketed the heavily agricultural North Carolina Piedmont.

By the time of her trip to Willowside, seventy-seven-year-old Frances Benjamin Johnston was well established as one of the nation's finest photographers. Growing up in a politically and socially well-connected, financially secure family in Washington, DC, Johnston had training as an artist at the Academie Julian in Paris that helped shape her cosmopolitan aesthetic. Returning home to the nation's capital to establish her own photography studio, after the turn of the century Johnston became one of the nation's leading portrait photographers whose celebrity subjects included Susan B. Anthony, Mark Twain, Booker T. Washington, Joel Chandler Harris, and five successive American presidents: Grover Cleveland, Benjamin Harrison, William McKinley, Theodore Roosevelt, and William Howard Taft.

In the first two decades of the twentieth century, Johnston shifted to landscape, garden, and historic architecture photography, gaining a top national reputation in these new subfields. By the mid-1920s, she increasingly focused on the historic architecture of the American South, which was disappearing rapidly through neglect or abandonment in one of the country's most impoverished regions. Johnston understood her work as a personal mission to preserve images of an important, vanishing part of American heritage. By 1940, she had accumulated more than 7,500 photographs of regional historic structures that she donated to the Library of Congress. There the images formed a substantial part of the nation's larger Historic American Building Survey special collection, accomplishing her intended preservation purpose. Fiercely independent, always single, immensely talented, and participating in powerful social, political, and business networks, Frances Benjamin Johnston was an acknowledged American master of photography.

During the mid-1920s, Johnston started her architectural photographic surveys with historic structures in Virginia and Lowcountry South Carolina. In the 1930s, she received a series of generous grants from the Carnegie Foundation to support and extend her preservation work to North Carolina and other southern states. Prominent University of North Carolina at Chapel Hill officials introduced Johnston to local contacts to identify subject buildings throughout the Tar Heel state. Through the university's alumni network, she likely met Charlotte Blake, Gastonia municipal librarian, and John O. Rankin, Gastonia municipal treasurer and businessman, who advised Johnston's preservation photography in Gaston County. Although a civic leader in Gastonia's exploding, textile-driven, New South economy, John O. Rankin grew up in the Rankintown rural community on his father James C. Rankin's farm. Having moved to Gastonia in 1903, John O. Rankin knew Willowside especially well because it formerly belonged to his grandfather, was his father's birthplace, and adjoined his father's family farm. As a member of one of the county's long-established families, John O. Rankin likely helped identify the entire list of Gaston County's historic buildings that Johnston photographed, including Willowside.

In the mid-1780s, Revolutionary war veteran William Rankin and his young widowed bride Mary Moore Campbell built and occupied a smaller log house, which sat directly behind where Willowside later would be situated. This log house was converted into a detached kitchen when the newer, larger Willowside was erected sometime prior to 1804. Covered with siding boards, Willowside was a one-and-a-half-story, hall-and-parlor log house with a full-length, one-story front porch. Around 1840, its upper half-story was extended to a full second floor. Over the years, several rear additions were added to bring the total to four bedrooms. In the early twentieth century, an interior kitchen was added to the back of Willowside, and the William Rankin log house became a storage outbuilding.

In the summer of 1938, probably in August, when Frances Benjamin Johnston came to Willowside, the Rev.

Frank Bisaner Rankin (John O. Rankin's half-uncle, who was sixteen years younger) and his family lived there. Frank B. Rankin inherited the ancestral farm from his father Col. Richard Rankin. The Frank Rankin family included fifty-year-old "Preacher" Rankin (as he was known locally), wife Oneta Battley "Neta" Rankin, and the two youngest of their five children still at home.

The Frank Rankin family essentially lived at Willowside in genteel poverty under rural conditions then typical but by today's standards primitive. They had no electricity, heated with firewood, and Neta Rankin boiled the laundry each week in huge cast-iron cauldrons in the backyard. With regular help from a Black housemaid, Neta Rankin's able domestic economy allowed the family to manage remarkably well on the modest income that her husband earned as Mt. Holly High School principal and math teacher, a long-term Presbyterian supply minister at various local churches, and landlord of several tenant farming families. Frank Rankin's decision to stay on the family farm and limit himself to local employment opportunities appeared increasingly countercultural and unambitious as textile manufacturing, commerce, and big-steeple Presbyterian churches flourished in southern towns and cities.

On her outing that day, Frances Benjamin Johnston took three photographs: two of Willowside and another of the William Rankin log house. Bright sunshine from the east falling on these buildings indicates Johnston worked in the morning or midday on a clear day. Positioning her camera in the front yard, she took one photograph at a wide angle that allows a complete view of the front and south side of the hall-and-parlor frame house. A second photograph, taken at closer range from the other side of the front yard, depicts with greater visual detail just the right side of Willowside's front facade with its attached porch.

The third photograph of the William Rankin log house (built c. 1785) is the most historically and architecturally significant and received a full-page illustration in Johnston's classic *The Early Architecture of North Carolina*.[1] Johnston wanted to document the structure's unusual chimney because of its rare pioneer construction technique. The chimney's base up to the shoulder was built using cheaper, larger native stones, while more expensive bricks were reserved for the finer masonry work from the shoulder to the top of its narrower stack.

Anyone with internet access can view Frances Benjamin Johnston's photos of Willowside and the William Rankin log house available online at the Library of Congress website. Conveniently, all of her photographs can be scanned at different magnifications, revealing more or less detail and simultaneously shrinking or enlarging image size. Like all of her historic architecture photos, the focus in Johnston's three local images is strictly the buildings, with the homeowners left out entirely to allow the viewer to concentrate solely on architectural character.

Despite Johnston's nearly exclusive focus on historic architecture, a few items crept into the photos that reveal the personal side of Frank B. Rankin's family. The attractive landscaping and neat appearance of Willowside's yard are tributes to Neta Rankin's skillful gardening. In the second photograph, which provides a closer view of the front porch, the family's spitz dog lies in the porch's shade and makes direct eye contact with the camera. In the more panoramic

---

[1] Chapel Hill: The University of North Carolina Press, 1941.

view of Willowside, using the highest magnification, the same dog can be seen lying behind the porch swing with its head down. Richard Rankin, the family's younger son, and eventually my father, who was then a recent high school graduate preparing to attend Davidson College, years later told me the dog's name. I regret long since forgetting it, and everyone else who knew the dog is dead. As a result, the obscure pet remains anonymous, but timeless, in Johnston's photo.

Taken as a closer shot to accentuate construction details, the picture of the William Rankin log house chimney also captures a small, charming aspect of the family's rural life. Without the photo, my father never would have had any reason to tell me that those were his homing pigeon boxes attached to the building's outside wall. Johnston's photograph unintentionally recorded a farm boy's delightful hobby.

The surrounding farmland is barely visible in only one of Johnston's photographs. In the background of the close-up photo of the front porch, a patch of cultivated fields briefly interrupts the tree line beside the house. Perhaps I spotted the field because I helped cut and load fescue hay bales there as a teenager. My best guess is that this grainy-looking portion of the photo was a recently harvested cotton field.

Frances Benjamin Johnston concentrated exclusively on the historic architecture of Willowside and the William Rankin log house in her photographs, and the resulting images are beautiful, timeless, tranquil, and peopleless. The family dog and pigeon boxes might have snuck into the pictures, but there is no hint of human drama. In contrast, contemporary photographer Walker Evans's famous images of tenant farmers near Greensboro, Alabama, in *Now Let Us Praise Famous Men* (1936) include people's strained faces, their worn work clothes, and even intimate shots of their sparsely furnished bedrooms. The struggle and pathos of everyday tenant farming life are apparent in Evans's photos. But not in Johnston's pictures. She excluded those who inhabited the place to produce plain, elegant architectural records.

Because Johnston's architectural photos avoid people, it is easy to view them without appreciating what was happening in the world around Willowside. By 1938, the forces of industrial manufacturing were coalescing as the primary source of local employment, and family farms were increasingly threatened by the rise of industrial agriculture with its emphasis on mechanization, productivity, wage labor, and single cash crops. Despite all these trends, local folks found it difficult to comprehend just how endangered family farming really was. The same year that Frances Benjamin Johnston photographed Willowside (1938), Mt. Holly High School had just over 100 male students enrolled. One-quarter of them belonged to the school's chapter of Future Farmers of America and imagined their adult lives as countrymen. By the late 1950s, such an agrarian vision was no longer viable. Textile manufacturing dominated Gaston County's economy, and family and tenant farming were vanishing. The disappearance of local agriculture was permanent.

Willowside lost its identity as a farm in the mid-1950s. The resident tenant farmers moved away, and their houses began to decay. After Frank Bisaner Rankin's death, his widow Neta Rankin moved to town. A few years earlier, their younger son, Dr. Richard Rankin, had overseen the demolition of the William Rankin log house because of minor termite damage. Oldest son, Frank Battley Rankin, a practicing attorney, occupied Willowside with his family when his mother left. He and his three sisters sold the rest of the farm property to their brother Richard Rankin. As a sideline from his principal occupation as a physician, Richard Rankin tried unsuccessfully for fifteen years to run a profitable beef cattle operation on the old Rankin property. During the summers of my late boyhood and early teenage years, I worked on our cattle farm. In the mid-1970s, my father finally gave up livestock farming. The physical collapse of the old Appalachian barn on the Willowside property in the early 1990s after years of neglect symbolized the final demise of our family farming.

Willowside was sold out of the family after my Uncle Frank Battley Rankin's death in 2000. I still own and live on family property that borders my ancestral homeplace on three sides, but there is no active farming happening on any Rankin lands today. Conservation easements on my land and other properties that belonged to my two sisters and other relatives ensure the surrounding landscape will always remain natural and not become another residential housing development. Even with the loss of farming, the permanent protection of so much of our family land is a great consolation.

The ultimate irony of Frances Benjamin Johnston's historic photographs of Willowside and the William Rankin log house is their prescience in depicting the structures strictly as historic architecture without any connection to the rural community. In the twenty years following Johnston's visit, the network of family farms, of which Willowside was an important unit, disintegrated. The lone exception was the

Richard Rhyne farm just to the north, which raises cattle and hay to the present, although Rhyne family members principally support themselves with outside employment.

Today, non-family members own and occupy Willowside and appreciate its historic character and beautiful natural setting. The surrounding Rankin family lands now comprise the Rankintown Nature Preserve and, along with other properties protected by the regional land trust, are part of the Stanley Creek Forest Conservation Area. The older woodlands on these lands steadily mature and gain biodiversity. Loblolly and white pines are planted in former fields. Growing wildwoods and tree plantations replace the lost rural world of which Willowside was a fixture. Not only are the many generations of Rankin farmers that animated Willowside gone, but so is the surrounding farming community. Only fading memories cling to acres that once grew crops. As a Rankin descendant who dwells on the property but works sixteen miles away as head of a school, I find that the loss of my family's complicated, beautiful farming leaves a hole. There is a ghostly quality to secluded living in a place that once teemed with farm workers and animals. Also completely lost is a vast store of farming knowledge acquired and passed down through the generations. I can't even milk a cow.

Frances Benjamin Johnston's vacant pictures were strangely prophetic. There are no more Rankin farmers. Even so, remembering my ancestors' rich agricultural heritage exerts a powerful influence that strengthens both my connection to and affection for this place. And boyhood summers spent on our cattle farm at least initiated me into the tail end of this vanishing way of life. For most of its history, this place belonged to farming people, and the old dog lying on the porch, a young boy's pigeon box, the cotton fields, and the myriad other country things were lovely expressions of that bygone era. After almost two centuries, Willowside survives as a historic architectural relic, but the rural world it occupied has largely disappeared.

The sources for this essay include Maria Elizabeth Ausherman, *The Photographic Legacy of Frances Benjamin Johnston* (Gainesville, FL: University Press of Florida, 2009); Bettina Berch, *The Woman Behind the Lens: The Life and Work of Frances Benjamin Johnston, 1864–1852* (Charlottesville, VA: University Press of Virginia, 2000); Frances Benjamin Johnston, *The Early Architecture of North Carolina: A Pictorial Survey* (Chapel Hill, NC: University of North Carolina Press, 1941), especially "William Rankin House, 1782," photograph, p. 13; and Frances Benjamin Johnston, "William Rankin House," three photographs available online, 1938, Carnegie Survey of the Architecture of the South, Library of Congress:
(1) https://www.loc.gov/pictures/collection/csas/item/2017888413/
(2) https://www.loc.gov/pictures/collection/csas/item/2017888414/
(3) https://www.loc.gov/pictures/collection/csas/item/2017888415/

2

A Partnership in an Ongoing Creation

My father always said if a cut on the surface of the earth was properly handled, it was like a cut on a man's body, and Nature would do wonders to heal it. —Jesse Stuart, "Earth Is His Book," in *From The Land*

For, behold, I create new heavens and a new earth; and the former shall not be remembered, nor come into mind. —Isaiah 65:17

My family has always belonged to the farm, and my land ethic grew out of this deep sense of belonging. Even as a small boy visiting my grandmother at our ancestral home Willowside, the profusion of old things constantly reminded me of earlier generations. Venerable trees grew in the yard. Worn tools lay scattered in the early Appalachian log barn. A gray, weathered corn crib and other antiquated log outbuildings sat around the main house. Horses grazed, oblivious to the automobile age. Old furniture and furnishing filled Willowside, purchased not at an antique store but instead organic to the place.

Through the years, stories about the farm accumulated, passed down, and initiated me into family lore. My aunts repeatedly speculated about which distant cousins stole the old flintlock pistol and the original king's grant deed while attending family reunions in the 1930s. Or told the tale about how in the 1810s as a boy, my great-grandfather and a trusted enslaved man drove a wagon to Charleston by themselves and brought back the Lebanon cedar sapling that grew into the giant specimen in the front yard. Or showed me which Willowside bedroom was the same one in which my great-grandfather, grandfather, and father were all born. The old homestead was a living repository of the family's past and, for someone like me with a strong historical bent, always inspired fascination and signified continuity and permanence.

Time spent at the farm during childhood and teenage years deepened my relationship with the place. My family lived six miles away in town, closer to my father's medical office, but we still spent a great deal of time at the farm. In 1961, my parents built "the cabin," a rustic retreat on a beautiful, wooded hill above Stanley Creek, about 400 yards the way the crow flies from Willowside. After Sunday church often spring through fall, we went to the cabin to have lunch and spend afternoons. Several years during summers, our family moved to the cabin for two weeks or so. The surrounding old-growth woods were ideal to explore. A few hundred yards below was a four acre-pond, full of bream and bass.

Starting in boyhood, my mother drove me to the farm every weekday in the summer to stay with farm overseer John Haggins and his country homemaker wife Rozella Haggins. My first cousin Cree Rankin, who lived right down the hill at Willowside and was a year older, walked up each morning to join us. We followed Mr. Haggins through his daily rounds, managing a beef cattle operation for my father, which in the summer largely revolved around cutting and baling hay for winter cattle feed. For the first few years, there was a strong element of babysitting, but eventually we grew into real farm hands. We tossed hay bales, strung barbed-wire fences, and did other chores.

Besides cattle, Mr. Haggins kept scores of game chickens, guinea fowl, an assortment of mixed-breed dogs, a pair of mules to plow his large garden, pigs to slaughter, a milk cow, my oldest sister's riding horse, and our bird dogs. Working at the farm introduced me to a lovely, vanishing way of life and also imprinted the place's particular geography. Getting my driver's license eventually took me away to other better-paying summer jobs.

During all these years, the farm offered good hunting and fishing. At various times, my father and I hunted squirrels, quail, and doves. Each type of game exposed us to different places. Squirrel hunts brought us into the old hardwoods around the cabin. Quail hunts happened along the edges of our fields and pastures. Labor Day dove shoots in harvested grain fields were social affairs involving perhaps twenty family members and friends. With the weather always hot, sweaty men gathered around beer coolers at the end of the shoot. In summertime, sometimes alone or with friends, I would fish for bream from the pond's dock using a cane pole and crickets. There are few things more thrilling than a plunging bobber. Occasionally, Mr. Haggins and my father took me bass fishing on the pond in a jon boat. In all these ways, the farm became known and loved.

When my father quit the cattle business in the late 1970s, the Hagginses moved away, and Dad rented the farm to a commercial Christmas tree grower. The house that the Hagginses lived in was rented to a new tenant who worked away from the property. Likewise, after repeated break-ins by teenage vandals, we rented the cabin to protect it. My Uncle Frank Rankin and his last wife lived at Willowside in retirement but did no farming. Although we still called the place "the farm," the description was an anachronism. It was no longer a working family farm. No one drew their primary livelihood from the place. Jewell Daniels, the Christmas tree grower, lived elsewhere, and his management of the tree farm brought him to the property, mainly seasonally. Our house renters weren't farmers. We still visited occasionally to interact with them, but otherwise we spent less time and were less vitally connected. My family's decision to abandon farming but retain property ownership was a variation on the larger national pattern of family farms disappearing from rural America.

In the late 1980s, when my first wife and I both joined the Queens College faculty in nearby Charlotte as chaplain and history instructor, respectively, we moved with our infant son to the cabin for about a year. This began a period when my relationship with our family property became more serious, as did the strong, persistent urge to better understand and care for the place. My emerging family land ethic expressed itself in several ways. Building an extensive trail system around the property gave greater access to and knowledge of the place. A specialized tool, called a "shrub buster," uprooted invasive autumn olive bushes that spread throughout the woods. Wildflower manuals identified the abundance of species growing around the cabin. Rescued wildflowers, transplanted from imperiled sites across the state, enriched plant diversity. Eventually, in the late 1990s, involvement in the local land trust movement led to a decade-long, successful effort to protect our family lands and other Stanley Creek properties. But among all my efforts, the most transformative and satisfying was the hands-on soil conservation and erosion control done over a span of two decades.

Plenty of spots and gullies needed healing. As in the rest of the Piedmont, careless farming practices caused widespread erosion—in this case, my family's carelessness. There were two major types of soil damage. One involved sheet erosion, in which entire layers of topsoil washed away leaving behind only red clay. The other was gully erosion, where unchecked, rushing water dug deep, v-shaped gashes in the red-clay earth. In at least two places, behind the former Haggins house and in the wooded cove that fed the pond, these gullies were enormous, more than twenty feet wide and twenty feet deep. For years, we dumped trash and waste into the gully near the Haggins house to fill the void, with limited success. Heavy rains flowing through the gully at the rear of the pond always turned the water an ochre color. Eroded spots were just open, ugly wounds in the earth. Every rain made them worse. The disturbing reality was that my family was to blame.

My discovery of soil conservation was wholly unanticipated. Our first Christmas at the cabin, I read a collection of essays on farming and land stewardship. One of the most interesting was by the gifted Kentucky writer Jesse Stuart, on how his father reclaimed and restored their abused, hill-country farmland. The Stuart farm had terrible erosion problems, including gullies so deep that young Jessie Stuart and his boyhood chums used cut saplings to pole vault across them for fun. Mr. Stuart's technique to repair eroding land was so simple and elegant that anybody could do it. He gathered sticks, brush, and branches and laid them tips up into the gullies. The deeper the gully, the more plant matter needed to fill it. This woody debris caught wild grass and other plant seeds and loose organic material, trapping them in place as they washed down the eroded surface. Then the seeds germinated, producing protective vegetation that covered the raw soil. The brush piles formed organic bandages over the exposed, wounded earth, enabling it to heal. Mr. Stuart called this "pertectin' the land." Reading Stuart's essay upset all my previous thinking. Didn't soil conservation require large-scale, dirt-moving equipment to construct contoured terraces to slow water flow and thus check erosion in fields and pastures? Surely, soil conservation wasn't something so manual, hands-on, and simple. Or was it?

My first foray into soil conservation was a simple experiment to see if the Stuart technique worked. That same Christmas, when it came time after the holiday to throw out our large cedar tree cut on the site, I took it over to the eroded bank on the state-maintained dirt road that ran through our property. There an exposed clay bank, stripped of all topsoil, formed a wide band about the same color as the red Hereford cows we once raised. Situated between a large pasture and the road bed, the bank was about fifteen feet high, 120 yards long, and moderately sloped. Draining water creased it at intervals, but there were no gullies. A few small, stunted pine saplings and scattered tufts of grass were the only things clinging to life in such a sterile environment, but otherwise the red clay was raw and bare.

About halfway up the eroded bank in one of the drainage creases, I placed our single Christmas tree horizontally with its top pointing up the slope so that the branches would catch as much draining water as possible. The discarded cedar looked lonely and somewhat odd lying by itself on the otherwise bare, eroded space. Time would tell whether or not our single tree would do any good. I was simultaneously hopeful and skeptical about the prospects.

The results that spring were astonishing. The prickly cedar needles and branches did their job well and trapped a variety of wild seeds that sprouted vigorously inside the dried, decaying Christmas-tree skeleton. In the middle of the otherwise completely denuded, bare bank sat a single green spot where the dead Christmas tree had grown a small vegetative oasis. *The Stuart technique for "pertectin' the land" really did work.* Seeing this natural wonder filled me with determination to cover every eroded spot and fill every gully on our property with brush and branches. This was something I could do largely with my own body—no specialized equipment required beyond a pickup truck and chainsaw. It was a healing vision not only for the land but also for myself, although I didn't know so at the time.

In 1990, my family moved to Charlotte to be closer to Queens College, and once again we rented the cabin. Even living fifteen miles away, however, my commitment to protecting our family land remained strong. Almost every Saturday I drove to the farm to spend the day working outside. Often, my young son accompanied me to play briefly before going to my parents in town, while I returned to work alone. During these first years, there was abundant forest debris left over from Hurricane Hugo, whose Category 4, eighty-mile-an-hour winds blew down trees and branches all over the property. A chainsaw cut up limbs and fallen trees too big to carry whole. Using the Stuart "pertectin' the land" technique, I lined gullies and eroded spots all over the property. I also occasionally rented a backpack leaf blower and filled dry-weather drainage beds with leaves to keep them from becoming gullies.

Besides Hugo's woody debris, discarded Christmas trees were the other main material used to reverse erosion. With a small trailer purchased for farm work, I easily collected about thirty trees from the curbs of surrounding Charlotte neighborhoods, storing them in my side yard. Then every Saturday I took a load of five or so to the farm to either be placed on eroded spots or stockpiled for future use. I also scavenged discarded Christmas trees from neighborhoods in nearby Stanley and Mt. Holly a week or so after the holiday and added them to my stockpiles. Occasionally, Mr. Daniels culled unattractive or unhealthy Christmas trees from those he had planted, and these were used as well.

By the late 1990s, I had progressed from my small trailer to a larger U-Haul truck rented for a single Saturday after the Christmas holidays to collect and transport discarded trees from Charlotte curbsides to the farm. For several years, my father-in-law helped me. So did my son from about age ten until he was in high school. The annual Christmas tree collection day became a much-anticipated ritual and adventure. In a busy city, even in neighborhoods with lower speed limits, grabbing free Christmas trees and tossing them in the back of the rental truck was dangerous and required caution to avoid passing vehicles. Because discarded Christmas trees were worthless, nobody cared that we took them. After driving to the farm and dumping the first load of Charlotte trees, we collected more from neighborhoods near our property. These were thrown on stockpiles I kept around the farm for later conservation work. A typical collection day produced more than 120 trees. Total rental and gasoline costs usually ran just over $100. Not counting my time and labor, the annual cost of my erosion control was minimal.

By the early 2000s, the attendant at the Gaston County solid waste landfill—one of my father's old patients—allowed me to come into the facility and load my U-Haul truck with discarded Christmas trees brought there from all over the county. With the landfill only about seven miles away from the farm, I could pick up four full loads of trees in a single day to replenish my stockpiles. This saved time and increased the number of trees collected for erosion control to nearly 200. Since restoring eroded land depended on an ample supply of old Christmas trees to create the protective layer, I could reclaim more land.

Repairing eroded soil was strenuous but deeply rewarding work. In winter months, I would load my truck bed with some of the stockpiled, dead Christmas trees deposited around our property and then drive as near as possible to an eroded area. Then I dragged the trees to a bare spot and placed them tips up, on their sides, and next to each other so the entire area was covered with a thick, solid blanket of dried Christmas trees. Small trees were easy to drag. But a full-bodied, eight-foot Christmas tree required substantial exertion. If any saplings were clinging to life on the eroded soil, these were positioned upright between the evergreen branches of the prone tree to receive sunlight, moisture, and nutrients and thus encourage better growth. The wonderful thing about covering an eroded section with old Christmas trees was the realization that nature would do the rest. Nothing else was needed. By the end of spring, grass and weeds were shooting up through gaps between desiccated evergreen branches and revegetating the bare earth beneath.

My erosion-repair work occurred over a period of two

decades and focused on the farm's most damaged places. An early project covered the eroded roadside bank where I conducted my first experiment with our Christmas tree. Next came a 1000-square-foot hillside with sheet erosion behind an old tenant-house site just north of Willowside. Here a farm road allowed easy access so that trees needed to be dragged less than twenty yards. Another reclamation project was a large drainage ditch just south of Willowside. There were many other smaller jobs. The same Stuart technique was employed in every case.

The largest effort of all was the massive pond cove gully. Driving on Old NC Highway 27 was the easiest way to reach this gully where it began as a small ditch before growing into a massive, raw ravine. Here the amount of brush needed to fill the cavity was enormous. Despite several years of work, I filled less than one half—perhaps ten feet—of the gully's deepest section. Nevertheless, there—just as in all other places where brush was carefully applied—the erosion halted where the woody debris was deposited, and the soil began to heal.

Repairing damaged land bound me more closely to the place and assumed a spiritual dimension, complimenting my Presbyterian faith in surprising ways. I had an abiding feeling that my work was part of a larger divine initiative in the ongoing process of creation. Over and over again, the scriptural passage from Isaiah 65:17, "Then I shall create new heavens and a new earth," came to mind. Similarly, I had a recurring vision of the hand of God sweeping up all the downed branches, debris, and leaf litter from the surface of the woodlands and whirlwinding them perfectly into place to cover and fill all the eroded spots on our property. This vision of a divine conservation whirlwind also included uprooting all the horrible autumn olive shrubs and other invasive plants and adding them to the larger, swirling mass of erosion-control filler—thus accomplishing two good purposes at once. If God was going to repair the whole earth, why not also eliminate all the invasive plants at the same time? As methodical and mundane as my work was, I became convinced I was a slow-motion, small-scale actor in this larger drama of re-creation, and the work was powerfully invigorating.

My sense of being a partner in an ongoing creation made me wonder whether soil conservation was just a metaphor for the way the Holy Spirit involved itself in other creative activities. Perhaps the Spirit amplified all human gifts used in ministering to others and to the creation. If so, people of faith are meant to use their human gifts for good purposes and leave the rest to God's sustaining power. I gained a greater appreciation for creativity as perhaps one of the most fundamental divine gifts along with faith, hope, and charity. The soil conservation done at the farm also made me keenly aware of widespread erosion elsewhere. Every time I passed an eroded spot in my car, seeing the ugly, wounded soil offended me. I wondered if the county or a new volunteer erosion control club should use the massive number of discarded Christmas trees collected each year to organize a systematic effort to restore eroded lands.

There was a redemptive quality to my soil protection that seemed profoundly Christian. In March 1998 while serving as Queens College's vice president for institutional advancement, I published a 700-word special feature in *The Charlotte Observer*'s editorial page titled "Meeting Christ in Creation's Wounds." My theme was the possibility that Christ's invitation to encounter him through ministering to the most marginalized people (Matthew 25:31-46) extended to the most damaged, abused landscapes. At the farm, my work made me keenly aware that I was redeeming land damaged through my ancestors' poor management. My soil conservation served as a reparation for past carelessness. Since my property was inherited, protecting the land also became a way of thanking both the preceding generations and the Creator.

Several unusual things happened during soil conservation that felt like revelations. Cleaning off a large table rock to use as a natural picnic area for my family, I realized that the thick, root-filled, organic mat covering the rock could be cut and rolled up just like carpet and then transferred to another eroded site to be used as protective covering. This is exactly what I did, and the organic mat proved to be an ideal natural dressing over the degraded ground beneath. Finding the organic mat on the table rock came as an unexpected gift.

On another occasion, I showed my conservation work at the pond cove gully to an uninitiated friend who asked what was stopping me from completely filling the eroded ravine. I explained that finding enough organic material nearby and placing it carefully in the gully was a daunting, time-consuming, laborious task. Several days later a massive, unseasonable, late spring ice storm came and filled the woods with broken branches. The area immediately adjoining the eroded ravine was literally covered with woody debris dropped by the storm. My rational side considered the strange weather event to be a freaky coincidence. But seen through the eyes of faith, I could only wonder whether the Creator was supplying what was needed to fill the ravine. Branches and sticks, not manna and quail.

The most powerful evidence of the way soil conservation work was transforming me was a recurring dream I began having. In the dream, I lay in an eroded gully, fully alive, with my body simultaneously distinct but also merging into the surrounding earth. Small saplings grew directly out of my torso and stabilized the soil. My body itself was the healing medium. In my interior dream life, soil conservation integrated me into the earth and involved me at the deepest, unconscious levels in the healing process. If there were such a thing as a Presbyterian "Green Man," I was becoming one. Each time I woke from this dream, I felt peaceful and, quite literally, rooted into our family land.

My soil conservation work continued until my early fifties. With my son occupied with high school athletics, social life, and then college, I labored alone. Not only was loading and dragging large Christmas trees exhausting, but the woods can be dangerous. Several times, I took spectacular falls, once, in particular, landing with a bone-jarring thud on the ground. While never seriously hurting myself, it occurred to me that if a jagged stump had been under me, the results could have been awful. Also, with passing years, recovering from the resulting soreness and muscle aches took longer and longer. After twenty years, it was time to recognize limits and stop soil conservation. Much had been accomplished.

The amazing thing about soil conservation is that, once initiated, the process sustains itself. Returning years later to places long ago covered with Christmas trees reveals improved landscapes, now mostly covered with grasses and young trees. A protective layer of vegetation hides the underlying red clay. Successional growth proceeds, and the habitat is healthier. The earth is healing. This may be my greatest legacy on the property.

After all these years, I wonder if something similar is still happening in my soul. Perhaps the healing process expressed in my earlier dreams continues deep within my interior life, beyond cognition—just as the revegetation of formerly eroded places proceeds out of sight. The enveloping earth more fully subsumes my body. What once were saplings, firmly rooted in my human frame, now are grown into large, beautiful trees. In rich, stable soil, native shrubs and wildflowers are protruding from my ears and eyes. And a prayer of praise rises from moss-crusted lips. A new heaven and earth are coming into being not only in a reclaimed landscape but also in my innermost self. Mediated through a loving relationship with our family land, the Divine Life has been quietly nurturing and enriching not just the soil but also my soul, all along.

The main source for this essay is my *Rankintown Notes: A Journal of Minding and Mending Family Land, 1991–2003* (Gastonia, NC: Richard Rankin, 2010). Also see Jesse Stuart, " Earth Is His Book," in Nancy P. Pittman, ed., *From The Land* (Washington, DC: Island Press, 1988).

3

Belonging to the Rock Wall

For those who live on old family property, no human activity stands alone or happens without precedents. Everything connects to the natural surroundings and to the earlier generations who lived there. These deep ties transform ordinary work into adventure, and the work itself retrieves memories from the well of history, marrying the inhabitant more tightly to the place.

That's what happened with the rock wall. The project grew out of a larger effort to renovate a house on a wooded lot at the end of our driveway that my wife and I bought as a rental property in 2019. The house was on a a three-acre outparcel that originally belonged to my family but became separated from the surrounding property in the late 1950s. About a decade earlier, my grandfather, the Rev. Frank Bisaner Rankin, had given the lot to his son Frank Battley Rankin, a young attorney and highly decorated World War II veteran, and his English war bride, Kathleen Cree, for their first home. A then young local contractor, Richard Loftin, built the modest, single-story frame house to the high standards that would distinguish his long building career.

With their family soon growing to four children, Frank and Kathleen Rankin lived in their first home for about a decade before relocating several hundred yards up the dirt road to the larger and older family homeplace Willowside. Frank Rankin then sold their first house to Melvin Farmer, a local taxi cab driver. Farmer lived there for the next twenty years, and his daughter and granddaughter occupied the place for another forty years. Mr. Farmer's granddaughter, who eventually inherited the property, then sold it back to us. We called it the Gatehouse because of the location at our driveway entrance.

The Gatehouse lot sits on the edge of Stanley Creek lowlands and then climbs steadily toward the crest of a high hill, crowned with scattered rock outcroppings. Because of the lot's slope, a concrete-block, step-back retaining wall was constructed in the original site preparation. The retaining wall was two feet high and sat four feet from the front of the house. Over the decades, gravity and the pressure of rainwater runoff tilted this wall, giving it an unattractive, lopsided appearance. Our handyman first suggested building a new concrete-block wall. But he quickly concurred with my idea of covering and reinforcing the original wall with native stone. Covering the existing wall with rock felt right because it honored both the place and its previous inhabitants. Sourcing the rocks from the surrounding hills satisfied a preference for a native, traditional building material—one close by and free. Gathering stones for the wall became major physical and emotional outlets while my wife and I quarantined during the Covid pandemic at our home just up the hill.

One reason a rock wall resonated so strongly was that it extended an older family tradition of stone masonry. The earliest example was the imposing stone fireplace and chimney of William Rankin house, a small, hewn-log structure built in the mid-1780s. This was the first home for my great-great-grandparents, and it stood immediately behind the larger, slightly later Willowside, our ancestral homeplace. The design of the original William Rankin fireplace's huge ten-by-four-foot opening and large stone hearth was straight out of the Middle Ages, complete with wrought-iron hangers to swing the cooking pots in and out. Although my father as a child played with his siblings inside the house's cavernous fireplace, as an adult he failed to appreciate either its historic or architectural significance. In the early 1950s, he tore down the whole structure because of minor termite damage—an action he later came to regret. Fortunately, among the several surviving pictures of the great fireplace and its exterior chimney, there is one full-page photograph by gifted Depression-era photographer Frances Benjamin Johnston that appears in the classic *The Early Architecture of North Carolina* (1941).

Another instance of family stone work, related to the older William Rankin house, was found at a place we called "the cabin." In 1961, my mother and father built this country retreat with a monumental stone fireplace as its centerpiece on a lovely hilltop site on farm property. Nine feet wide by eight feet high, with a chimney stack extending eight feet above the roof line, the fireplace was constructed with stones salvaged from the demolition of the old William Rankin house hearth and chimney. Some of the hearthstones are two feet by one foot in size and show quarry marks. In the late 1780s, my ancestor William Rankin gathered these very stones. Or perhaps he purchased or bartered the largest rocks from a local quarry and transported them by wagon to the site. About fifteen years ago, my wife and I moved into the renovated and expanded cabin, renaming it "Willow Hill" to reflect the site's topography and to allude to close-by, historic Willowside. At Willow Hill, the great stone fireplace remains a monumental and compelling feature that evokes strength and permanence. On an almost unconscious level, the fireplace functions as a powerful symbol of the family's attachment to this place and my own continuity with our past.

Rock walls are not commonplace in the North Carolina Piedmont. Unlike glacial New England, where stones litter the landscape, rocks here are scattered and often partly buried, thus requiring considerable labor to gather and transport to a building site (as I quickly learned). Even so, there are several splendid examples around old church cemeteries. The closest is about three miles east of the Gatehouse where a group of Irish gold miners established St. Joseph's Catholic Church in 1843. There a handsome, substantial stone wall about three feet high encloses the surrounding churchyard cemetery. Perhaps miners built the wall with the rock spoils from their mine tunnels.

With all these examples of historic rock masonry as precedents, it was time to start gathering stones. Instead of beginning the search at the Gatehouse, I headed up the hill on an old logging road to the rock outcroppings. However, less than a hundred yards into my hike, the road became choked with a terrible invasive shrub, autumn olive, making it impassable. Swinging around the road's ugly, foreign-shrub tangle took me into the clearer, adjoining woods. This unplanned detour brought me to a familiar, long-abandoned tenant house site about halfway up the hill where only a few scattered bricks and stones mark earlier habitation. Here grows the largest post oak tree on the property. The giant measures 171 inches in circumference or 4.5 feet in diameter at breast height, approximately 90 feet in height, and has a crown spread of roughly 75 feet. Its overall big tree score is 336, combining diameter, height, and canopy size. At about 20 feet, the main trunk forks into two branches, and the bottom 30 feet of the tree are covered with huge knobs formed where enormous limbs have broken off and then healed through the years. The tree trunk's base includes gnarled top roots that, in several cases, extend ten feet before disappearing underground.

Since my last visit several years earlier, the site had become littered with fallen limbs, overblown small trees, and invasive autumn olive plants. Even with the clutter and debris on the forest floor, the great tree was magnificent and seemed to welcome me as a guest into its quiet mystery. What was it about that place that was so enthralling? The grandeur of the Great Oak? The palpable sense of earlier habitation? Whatever it was, a sublime and tranquil mood came over me that lasted long after the hike was over. That evening I struggled to articulate the experience to my wife.

The visit to the Great Oak that afternoon was necessarily brief because my destination was the hilltop rock outcroppings. Rejoining the logging road beyond the autumn olive tangle led me to another familiar place. Maybe thirty years earlier, I had named it "the Indian High Rock" to fire the imagination of our young children. The name came from one of the largest boulders there: a large, flat table rock, with perhaps a twenty-by-ten-foot surface that, until about a decade ago, served as a picnic area for our family. With our children grown and gone, remembering happy times and realizing how quickly time passed made me wistful.

Choosing the name for Indian High Rock came without

any real evidence, other than a strong hunch, that the spot was indeed a Native American site. The size of the table rock and the dramatic view down the steep north-facing slope made me confident that others had been drawn there before. Who could resist the desire to stand on such a splendid natural platform and survey the vista below? Surely through the millennia, Piedmont People must have visited this place often and gazed down the stone-studded ravine. The natural grandeur of the place was a common inheritance that linked us to those original inhabitants.

Today, the primary purpose at the Indian High Rock was rock hunting, and as hoped, there were some loose, scattered stones. But surprisingly few. Most were partly buried, and extracting them would require considerable prying and digging. Then would come wheelbarrowing several hundred yards down the hill to an access point at the driveway and loading the rocks into the truck bed to make the short drive to the Gatehouse. This job was not going to be quick or easy. Finishing my rock reconnaissance that afternoon, I headed back to the driveway and up the hill to our house. At that moment, I had no idea how much the search for rocks was going to reconnect me to the Great Oak, the Indian High Rock, and several other special places on the property. On old family property, the most mundane job integrates the caretaker into the place and its past.

For the following few weekends, I split time accumulating rocks on the Gatehouse hill and cleaning up around the Great Oak. The two activities complemented each other. The work also produced an exciting discovery. About twenty yards above the great tree sat a previously unknown stone fire pit—which was old, perhaps ancient—right in the middle of a small rock outcropping. Who had constructed this fire pit? Native Americans? Long hunters? The inhabitants of the abandoned house site? The work at the Great Oak was revealing new mysteries and expanding my mental boundaries of the Gatehouse property to include the Great Oak and the Indian High Rock. These three places were becoming continuous and interrelated in my mind.

The work around the Great Oak also inspired a new vision for the place as a campsite for my young grandson, his father, and me. With the great tree as a dramatic central focus, the old fire pit as a place to roast hot dogs and marshmallows, and the flat area around the old house site as a perfect spot to pitch a tent, the site really was the ideal woodland retreat for the Rankin boys. The search for rocks was bringing the whole hill alive in my imagination and actions as I realized its potential for family recreation.

My rock search revealed that gullies were often choice spots as draining water washed away soil leaving exposed rocks. After noticing this phenomenon in several places, a flash of insight came: if draining water did this to a gully, what had nearby Stanley Creek done to its creek bed? That weekend I put on waders, called my dog Tuck, and headed to Stanley Creek to look for rocks. It was late August as we entered the woods about thirty yards from the Stanley Creek bridge and another fifty yards on a direct line to the Gatehouse. In summer heat, the cool creek water felt pleasant as it spilled over my waders and soaked me almost to the waist; the deepest part of the channel was perhaps three feet. We only waded fifty yards, crossing a small beaver dam, before seeing a rocky shoal littered with several hundred stones and rocks of various sizes and shapes. Many lay exposed in shallow water with small rapids rushing around them. Others were partly buried. The rocky shoal contained just the sort of large concentration of rocks in a confined area that I needed. The only problem would be transferring the heavier rocks from the creek bed up the steep, eight-foot-high banks to level ground. There I could wheelbarrow them to the truck. With the inspection completed, we headed back to Willow Hill.

The next weekend Tuck followed me to the shoal, and I spent half a day tossing rocks from the creek bed up onto level ground above the southeast bank. The smallest suitable stone was twice as large as a man's fist—anything smaller was too small for the rock wall. The largest I could heave was perhaps the size of a loaf of bread. It was strenuous but pleasant work. Being at the shoal with small rapids on each side of the creek made me wonder whether Native Americans once constructed fishing weirs at this exact place. After throwing over a hundred rocks up the bank to level ground, I drove the truck to a point on the main road closest to the rock pile, cut a fifty-yard trail through the white pines to the creek, and wheelbarrowed eight or ten loads to my truck bed. The drive to Gatehouse, where the rocks were unloaded, was no more than 300 yards.

Only one challenge remained at the rocky shoal. Left behind at the site were perhaps fifty larger rocks too heavy to hurl up the high bank. How could they be moved easily to the Gatehouse? As I brainstormed over the next several days, an intriguing idea came to me. My stepdaughter had purchased a small, light blue kayak to paddle in and explore our farm pond several years earlier. With her now grown and living in Rhode Island, the kayak sat idle, collecting dust in a storage shed. Could the kayak be used as a barge, with its seat a storage compartment for the larger rocks, and then floated down the creek to an easier place to unload? It was a creative, unproven scheme that just might work, and I was eager to test it.

The following Saturday, I drove the truck down the driveway to a point nearest the creek and dropped off the kayak. Pruning hooks, a handsaw, and a chainsaw were brought to dismantle the beaver dam blocking direct access to the shoal. Tuck would be too rambunctious and unpredictable around a chainsaw, so he was left behind. Stowing the tools in the seat of the kayak, I pulled the craft upstream against a moderate current by a leader rope tied to the front. Because certain parts of the creek bottom were slippery, I hesitated using the chainsaw. Luckily, I was able to open up one end of the beaver dam with just the pruning hooks and handsaw. The strong volume of water pouring through the dam's gap was enough to easily float the kayak to and from the shoal.

After pulling the kayak up to the shoal and grounding it on a small sandbar, now came the plan's moment of truth. I loaded a half-dozen large rocks in the kayak seat, pushed off the sandy bottom into the current, and—just as hoped—it floated effortlessly down the stream as I waded alongside. It was only thirty yards to a point where the banks were four feet high and more gently sloping. As I waded here into a shallow branch joining the main channel, the kayak's weight grounded it firmly to the bottom. In this way, repeated trips back and forth from the shoal brought all the large rocks to the branch's shallow staging area.

Unloading the large rocks from the shallows was a two-stage process. The first step was to put them on a small, natural dirt shelf halfway up the bank that could be reached from the creek. Climbing up the bank to anchor myself against a fallen tree trunk, I then heaved all the larger rocks a few feet above to level ground. From start to finish, the whole process took less than two hours. Within another hour, all the rocks had been wheelbarrowed to the truck bed and driven less than 200 yards to the Gatehouse. My ingenuity in using the kayak gave me a rush of accomplishment and satisfaction. Perhaps I was the first human being ever to float rocks down Stanley Creek. A pioneer and pathfinder on a modest scale.

After more than a month's work on the Gatehouse hill and in Stanley Creek, rocks often occupied my thoughts and dreams. Every discovery triggered new ideas. The success of the Stanley Creek project made me wonder if a creek and woods behind Gaston Day School where I worked—sixteen miles away—also held rocks. Access was easy. Driving the truck across a vacant school field would bring it to the head of the cross-country team's trail. The trail ran over the nearby creek on a makeshift bridge and wandered through the woods on school grounds. The idea of importing rocks from non-family property contradicted my original plan to use only homegrown material. Even so, any Gaston Day rocks would come from a place central to my professional life. Besides, finding rocks was hard work, and I was more than ready to compromise location for convenience.

On a Friday after school in early September, I hiked out to the school's cross-country trail to hunt for rocks. Staying on the path across the creek with the wheelbarrow, I found perhaps twenty scattered rocks around what was once the fireplace of an old house site now overgrown with twenty-five-year-old poplar and pine trees. My only hesitation was that scavenging diminished the remains of a formerly inhabited place. The rocks themselves were residue not only of a collapsed chimney but also human history. Disturbing a long-abandoned house site made me wonder if I was just a lesser version of a modern-day tomb raider. On the other hand, the idea of repurposing these rocks forced me to reflect on the original residents and be grateful for their labor. Nobody else knew or cared about the abandoned rocks. Also, my father's precedent in recycling the William Rankin fireplace stones into the cabin's fireplace came to mind. I decided it was alright to take the rocks.

Over the next several weeks, I collected more than 200 rocks from the school site and transported them to the Gatehouse. The labor gave a much more intimate understanding of the school's property and a better appreciation of its natural character. And a new kinship with and respect for those who had once lived at the house site. They were no longer completely overlooked or forgotten.

Just as earlier searches had generated new ideas for places to hunt for rocks, finding rocks off the cross-country trail called to mind another spot back home not previously considered. It was a wet-weather drainage on the rear edge of the property behind Willow Hill that I thought I remembered having exposed rocks. The next Saturday morning, Tuck and I headed back to the site on another old logging road, and sure enough, there were scores of rocks strewn along a thirty-yard segment of the steep drainage bed. Here the tactic was first to consolidate the dispersed rocks into a small staging area on the path, then wheelbarrow the heap to the truck at the logging road's end. Gathering them took only about an hour. It was easy carrying rocks downhill from points above the trail. But lugging rocks from below required hard, awkward effort, which caused several slips and stumbles. After depositing all the rocks at the staging area, the work followed the usual pattern: wheelbarrow, truck, Gatehouse. The rock pile there had grown considerably to perhaps more than 700.

After several months of hard work and accumulating my rock pile at the Gatehouse site, the actual construction of the wall was straightforward and easily completed on two successive Saturdays. Using the old concrete block wall as a core, I stacked the new stones to form an attractive shell that reinforced and covered the old wall. Positioning the rocks was like assembling a three-dimensional jigsaw puzzle—largest rocks on bottom, smallest on top. The wall stood about three feet high on its lower face when finished. I dressed the upper side with loose dirt to form a dam to divert water draining down the slope away from the house. I also dug two French drains, one above and one below the rock wall, to drain excess water away from the house. The stacked rocks cover the buckled wall, and the French drains form an effective water barrier. Even with all its physical challenges, finishing the project made me realize how much gathering rocks meant to me and how much I was going to miss the accompanying adventure. The whole process deepened my relationship with the land and its history.

My rough-hewn rock wall serves a plain, practical purpose. But the wall also functions as a marker whose significance reaches back in time and out into the surrounding landscape. The work reminded and reintroduced me to those who preceded me on the land: Native Americans, gold miners, tenant farmers, and my ancestors. The construction material echoes the William Rankin house and cabin fireplaces, the rock wall around the St. Joseph's cemetery, and the long-abandoned house site at school. The rocks themselves connect and unite the Great

Oak, the Indian High Rock, Stanley Creek, and all the other places that were sources. The structure embodies my physical labor, creativity, and the adventure that accompanied rock gathering. All these elemental qualities endow the wall with great emotional meaning and make it a monument to this place, its past, and my membership in both.

Developed over many generations, deep affection for an old family place has the tendency to transform ordinary work—like rock wall building—into a kind of art. The rich historical and natural context binds the artist/worker more closely to the place and its past. Affection, imagination, family history, interaction with the natural environment, native materials, and labor all converge to create a profoundly satisfying and unifying experience. All these elements form powerful bonds between the artist/worker, the work project, the natural surroundings, and the living and the dead who once resided there. Such work expresses and cultivates a deeper sense of belonging to family land.

4

In the Company of the Rankin Oak

The massive southern red oak amazed everyone who saw it. The tree was situated about twenty yards south of the fine frame house that James C. Rankin and his wife Susan Ellen Davenport Rankin built shortly after the Civil War. Already perhaps 300 years old, the tree grew there possibly before 1587 when the first English New World settlement, the Lost Colony, was established on North Carolina's coastal Roanoke Island. In 1870, the great oak likely measured well over four feet in diameter, was maybe sixty feet in height, and possessed an enormous canopy. Over the next hundred years, it attained even greater size before finally succumbing to old age. Residents could not help but celebrate and admire something so grand, ancient, and beautiful. Eventually, the giant hardwood gained official recognition as the largest of its species in the southeastern United States, becoming known as the Rankin Oak.

James and Susan Rankin were the last members of their family to live next to the great tree. For reasons now lost to history, their son Edgar and his wife Lola Rankin moved their family to Chapel Hill 150 miles to the east sometime before 1896. When they relocated, Edgar Rankin, who died shortly afterwards, presumably rented the James C. Rankin homeplace to its first tenant farmers. After Edgar's death, his wife Lola and their three children, Estelle, Ralph, and Susan Rankin, stayed in Chapel Hill. As an adult, Susan

Rankin married and moved to Rocky Mount in eastern North Carolina. Estelle Rankin remained single. Ralph Rankin married late in life and had no children. Both Estelle and Ralph Rankin lived together in Chapel Hill for the rest of their lives. There Ralph achieved a distinguished fifty-year career at the University of North Carolina's Extension Office. As an adult, absentee owner, he employed the tenants who worked the old James C. Rankin farm for his family. Although Ralph and Estelle were in Chapel Hill, their connection to the old homeplace and the great tree remained strong.

In 1926, widower Jerome "Rome" Allison moved into the James C. Rankin house with his four children to tenant farm for Edgar Rankin's widow and children. Two years after moving to Rankintown, Allison married Nanny Robinson and added her two children to their new household. The Allisons would live there for the next decade. The giant oak's influence on the Allisons was significant, and daughter Mamie remembers the tree fondly. The backyard was situated under the oak's spreading branches that extended almost 120 feet. The Allisons swept the yard clean to the dirt each week with a broom made of dogwood branches, a custom of that day. Rome Allison placed a large, flat rock between two of the tree's above-ground roots as a favorite seat where he rested from his farm work. The girls played house, hopscotch, jump rope, and jump the plank. The boys played baseball and marbles. Everyone pitched horseshoes. Beans were strung and hung out to dry. Laundry was washed in the big wash tub each Monday. In summer, homegrown peaches were washed in the same washtub. Family members chose different tasks in preparing the peaches: peeling, pitting, and slicing the fruit to be eaten as preserves during the winter. All this happened under the huge tree that now had attained an impressive girth of more than five feet at a grown man's breast height.

The great tree also provided a shady stage and a verdant backdrop for outdoor parties. During the summer, the Allisons invited friends and relatives to celebrate Nanny Allison's birthday under the tree. Sawhorses and planks were covered with white starched tablecloths, making strong, attractive tables that held fried chicken, chicken and dumplings, assorted garden vegetables, baskets of homemade rolls, sweet potato custards, and chocolate cakes. A new tin tub was filled with fresh, cold lemonade. On most Saturday nights, friendships and romances grew under the tree as young people gathered for yard parties. In all likelihood, the giant tree had sheltered similarly happy occasions ever since James C. and Susan Rankin first moved there after the Civil War.

Ralph Rankin regularly visited the Allisons, following a well-established routine. On Friday, he traveled from Chapel Hill to Charlotte where he would spend the night. The next morning he arrived at Rankintown early for breakfast. Expecting his visit, the Allisons brought out the white tablecloth and prepared their very best meal. After discussing farm matters, Rankin enacted an old landowner's ritual and walked the boundaries of his family property. He felt great affection for the place, and he particularly loved its trees. No tree on the property was more prized than the big oak. How often did Ralph Rankin walk up to the tree and touch it? Or did he simply gaze at it admiringly and reflect on happy, past occasions spent under its stately branches?

For all the great southern red oak's life thus far, it was strictly a local phenomenon, known only to a close circle of landowners and their tenants and neighbors. But that changed in 1937 when William Chambers Coker and Henry Roland Totten, two of the University of North Carolina's most famous botanists, became aware of and described the Rankintown oak in the second edition of their masterwork, *Trees of the Southeastern States.* Coker, a South Carolina native, joined the botany faculty at the University of North Carolina in 1902 and stayed there for fifty-one years. Totten, a Mecklenburg County native, was a graduate student under Coker and immediately joined the Botany Department faculty in the late 1910s. Both Coker and Totten had long, distinguished teaching and research careers that produced a multitude of publications.

Almost certainly, Ralph Rankin read the first edition of *Trees of the Southeastern States* when it was published in 1934 and realized that his family's southern red oak might be as big or bigger than the ones mentioned in the text. By the mid-1930s, Rankin, Coker, and Totten had been colleagues at the university for twenty-five years. They surely were strong acquaintances and perhaps genuine friends. One can imagine Rankin reading the reference work on Southeastern trees and taking a tape measure with him on his next visit to the old homeplace to at least record the oak's girth. Rankin must have informed the two university botanists about the tree's size. Whether Coker and Totten traveled to see the great tree themselves is unknown. Maybe they did. Or maybe the two plant experts deputized Ralph Rankin as their field assistant and gave him specific instructions and guidance in how to measure all the dimensions of his specimen. Whoever did the measuring, the results were definitive and made their way into the second edition.

Here is what *Trees of the Southeastern States* says: "The

large 'Rankin Oak' four miles northwest of Mt. Holly, N.C., has a diameter of 5 feet 6 inches four and a half feet from the ground and a limb spread of 123 feet." While no height is listed for the Rankin Oak, pictures suggest it was between sixty and eighty feet tall. Coker and Totten listed two other large specimens of southern red oaks in their book. One grew in Chapel Hill with a diameter of five feet six inches, measured five feet above ground. Another southern red oak in Cheraw, South Carolina, was five feet three inches in diameter five feet above ground. No mention of canopy size is made for either of the two trees, suggesting the Rankin Oak's crown spread was notably large. No other southern red oaks are discussed in *Trees of the Southeastern States*. These three were presumably the largest known to exist. Since then, many larger red oaks have been discovered. Today the national champion southern red oak in Upson County, Georgia, dwarfs the Rankin Oak. It is 8 feet 10 inches in diameter, 123 feet tall, and 152 feet in crown spread. Even so, the Rankin Oak was an enormous tree.

After the publication of *Trees of the Southeastern States* in 1937, the Rankin Oak was official. The most respected book about regional trees had named, measured, recorded, and identified it. In the world of Southeastern trees, the Rankin Oak was certified. But its new celebrity did little to change life on the farm. Visitors always marveled when they first saw the tree. But these folks came to visit the Allisons, not the tree. No tourists flocked to it. The Rankin Oak's main influence was still on the lives of those who lived under its massive branches.

In 1936, a new family of tenant farmers, the Huffstetlers, replaced the Allisons and moved into the old James C. Rankin house. The Huffstetlers included husband

George, his wife Mary, their three daughters Nell, Margie, and Janie, and a son Lytle. Ralph Rankin continued to oversee the property and make regular visits. As it had for the Allisons, the big tree remained a focus for social, recreational, and work activities. The Huffstetler children played many of the same games. The base of the tree became the girls' dollhouse with the aboveground roots, tapering into the trunk, acting as walls to create separate dollhouse rooms.

Two momentous occurrences happened while the Huffstetlers lived at Rankintown. The first was a catastrophic fire in 1938 that consumed the James C. Rankin house. For a number of years, one of the chimneys had pulled away from the frame of the house. Ralph Rankin patched this opening with tin, but the repair left the chimney still vulnerable. Somehow sparks found a crack there, caught the house on fire, and burned it to the ground. In response to the disaster, Ralph Rankin built a smaller, new frame house on the original site, and the Huffstetlers occupied their new quarters. The great oak survived the fire unscathed.

About four years later, a loud crack awakened the family in the middle of the night. Lightning had struck the big tree, ripping a gash up and down the length of the trunk. Concerned that it would die, Ralph and Estelle Rankin hired tree surgeons from nearby Mt. Holly to attend the great oak. Young workers climbed the tree, cleaned out the wound, and packed it from top to bottom with concrete. The Rankins paid $100 to repair the tree, a considerable sum in 1942. The great oak survived the calamity and stayed healthy.

For as long as the Huffstetlers remained at the farm, the Rankin Oak acted as a focal point in their lives. But in the late 1950s, they left Rankintown to become tenant farmers in southwestern Gaston County. They may have been the last tenants on the Rankin property. Family farming declined sharply in Gaston County and throughout the country in the 1950s. Ralph Rankin shifted his focus away from tenant farming to timber management. At this point, the fate of the Rankin Oak became unclear. Eventually the tenant house stood vacant, and the Rankin Oak stood alone. Rankintown itself disappeared as a rural community.

No one is certain when the Rankin Oak finally died. Perhaps the late 1960s. Perhaps the 1970s. Since neither Ralph nor Estelle Rankin had any children, their sister Susan Fountain's children, who never lived at Rankintown, inherited the property. Youngest child and only son, Richard Tilman Fountain Jr., a successful Rocky Mount attorney, assumed responsibility for the family property and visited occasionally. Although one of his sisters knew about the Rankin Oak, he did not.

Apparently sometime in the 1980s, Nell and Margie Huffstetler (married names Crouse and Faires, respectively) visited the old homeplace and photographed the enormous dead tree, a twenty-foot snag covered with kudzu vines. The Rankin Oak was rotting away, and those who remembered it were passing away. Mamie Allison Cole (b. 1922), Nell Huffstetler Crouse (b. 1929), and Margie Huffstetler Faires (b. 1939) retained cherished memories of growing up under the Rankin Oak. They are the last living witnesses who knew the tree well. Without them, the Rankin Oak would survive only as a reference in *Trees of the Southeastern States* with no one to identify precisely where it had once stood, other than "four miles northwest of Mt. Holly, N.C." The great tree was vanishing from local memory.

Spending a considerable amount of time growing up on family land that adjoined the old James C. Rankin property (James was my half-great-uncle), I knew absolutely nothing about the Rankin Oak. In the late 1990s, my involvement with the Catawba Lands Conservancy finally introduced me to its story. After my wife and I took a conservation easement on seventy-one acres of family land on Stanley Creek— creating the Rankintown Nature Preserve—the conservancy identified the adjoining property belonging to the heirs of siblings Estelle and Ralph Rankin and Susan Rankin Fountain as a key conservation target. At 506 acres, this was an enormous property in the Piedmont less than fifteen miles from Charlotte. The natural quality was perhaps even more remarkable than its size. In 2000, the North Carolina Natural Heritage Program designated the Rankin heirs property (hereinafter called the Estelle Rankin heirs property) as one of the finest natural areas in the state.

One outgrowth of the Catawba Lands Conservancy's work on Stanley Creek was a serious community study. As part of his graduate work, former conservancy staff member Gabriel Cummings examined how Stanley Creek and three other rural North Carolina communities responded to urban and suburban development pressures. As research for his published project, called *Perspectives on the Land*, Cummings interviewed Stanley Creek residents and landowners, including me. He presented his findings to the Stanley Creek community in a special program at the First Presbyterian Church, Stanley, on Sunday, September 21, 2003. Many longtime residents attended, including Ed Wallace, a local naturalist who lived about two miles northwest of the Estelle Rankin heirs property on Old North

Carolina Highway 27. My wife and I went too.

This was the first time Ed Wallace and I ever met. Conversation was easy because of our shared fascination with Stanley Creek's natural history. We had barely gotten started when Wallace asked if I knew that the largest southern red oak in the state had grown on the old Estelle and Ralph Rankin property. Never having heard of the Rankin Oak, I was momentarily skeptical at Wallace's question. But he instantly produced a third edition copy (1945) of *Trees of the Southeastern States* and showed the reference to the Rankin Oak. Wallace knew that the tree was located somewhere near the old James C. Rankin homestead, but not exactly where. Over the following weeks, I reached out to several older relatives, and they had only vague knowledge of the tree. I pursued the matter no further at the time.

Four months after the *Perspectives on the Land* event, the Catawba Lands Conservancy finally concluded its acquisition of the Estelle Rankin heirs property. The conservancy had spent four years securing the necessary funding for the purchase. The State of North Carolina's Ecosystem Enhancement Fund provided the money, and family members agreed to sell. Richard Fountain remarked that his family decided to participate in a conservation sale in part because Aunt Estelle Rankin would have wanted it that way. The old James C. Rankin home site now belonged to the conservancy, and the whole property was renamed the Stanley Creek Forest.

The Catawba Lands Conservancy's work on Stanley Creek generated considerable publicity in local newspapers. Mamie Allison Cole, whose family had been tenant farmers at the old James C. Rankin homeplace, next to the Rankin Oak, was elated to learn about protection of the property.

Now in her early eighties, Cole had spent her entire life within reasonably close proximity to Rankintown, and for more than the last thirty years lived about five miles away in her home outside Stanley. The protection of the Stanley Creek Forest inspired Cole, and she began to write a number of wonderfully rich and detailed articles recollecting her life as a member of a tenant family on the Rankin farm. Hard work, rich family life, bountiful nature, and happy times were repeated themes in her writing. A few of these essays were published in local newspapers and one in the conservancy's newsletter, and she shared others with friends. Because Cole appreciated my role in Stanley Creek land protection and my interest in local history, she also shared her unpublished stories with me. Since my father was her family's physician and delivered her two children, she already knew him well. Cole was also a distant Rankin relative. As a result of all these mutual interests and connections, Mamie Cole became a close friend.

For the next nine years, my interest in the Rankin Oak receded and lay dormant. However, despite other priorities, the Stanley Creek Forest remained terribly important. In November 2007, after several years of dreaming about what it would be like to live there, my wife and I renovated, enlarged, and moved into a home originally built as a retreat by my parents on our family land. All the while, Mamie Cole stayed vitally interested in Rankintown's past, occasionally sending more of her writings and encouraging me to focus my own historical work on the same topic. About two years ago, I began to do just that, spending significant time researching old family deeds and records. As part of that research, I also interviewed both Mamie Allison Cole and Nell Huffstetler Crouse to capture their recollections of tenant farming life from 1926 to the late 1950s. The Rankin Oak naturally came up in their stories.

Even with this accumulating body of related material, I still was not focused on the Rankin Oak. All that changed suddenly over the 2012 Labor Day Weekend when I read Jim Robbins's *The Man Who Planted Trees*. The book tells the story of David Milarch, a northern Michigan nurseryman, who had a near-death experience in 1991 and then, soon after, came to believe supernatural beings visited him and communicated his new divine destiny: to clone the nation's oldest and largest trees and use the resulting, genetically superior tree stock to withstand the onslaught of global warming. As fantastic as Milarch's vision seemed, he pursued it with a singleness of purpose and, against great obstacles, succeeded in making it a reality over the next twenty years. With growing support from the scientific establishment, Milarch assembled a team of experts who have successfully cloned many champion trees. These include giant redwood stumps cut down early in the twentieth century—the living matter for cloning taken from the shoots and suckers growing out of the stump's base.

Reading about Milarch's ability to clone trees from living stumps, a thought flashed into my mind: could it be possible that the Rankin Oak survived as a living stump with shoots and suckers suitable for cloning? I laid down the book, pulled on hiking boots, and headed through the woods with my dog Tuck toward the old James C. Rankin house site. My mission was to try to find what remained of the Rankin Oak. My wildest hope was that the great tree might live on as a shoot or sucker sent up from its still living roots. The last 100 yards of my short hike took me through a tangle of briars and weeds that had grown up around the old house site—now nothing more than a couple of dilapidated brick chimneys. I picked my way through the prickly vegetation searching for a big stump close by. Amazingly, I found the remains of a huge tree—almost completely decomposed and with a stump hole at least ten feet across. A twelve-foot section of the rotting trunk still remained on one side of the stump hole, preserved because it had managed to land in such a way as to lie mostly off the ground. Around much of the hole, a thin bark shell survived, creating a broken wooden crown. The stump was thoroughly dead, with absolutely no living matter. Surely though, this had to be the last vestiges of the Rankin Oak. What else could it be?

Heading back home with Tuck from our adventure, I wondered how to be sure that the stump hole was what remained of the Rankin Oak. Later that day, an answer finally occurred to me. At least two living witnesses, Mamie Cole and Nell Crouse, could confirm whether I had found the Rankin Oak's last remains. The prospect of cloning the tree was no longer viable. But even if the great tree was dead and nearly gone, Cole and Crouse could identify where it once stood, and they would enjoy visiting their old homeplace and reminiscing about their earlier lives there. We could have a Rankin Oak reunion and invite everyone who had known the tree to revisit its location and celebrate its past. The idea of a tree reunion was both whimsical and exciting. My more conventional side imagined the response of several practical friends. Why in the world would anyone care about a big, dead, long decayed tree? Nevertheless, the more I thought about the possibility of a Rankin Oak reunion, the more I liked it.

Ignoring doubts and reservations, I contacted those who might be interested in the tree reunion. Sharon Wilson,

Conservancy Land Protection Coordinator, was enthusiastic and offered to bring an ATV to transport older individuals to the site. She gave permission to hold the event on Saturday, October 19, 2012. Nell Crouse and Mamie Cole were next. Crouse was very excited and told me that she had a younger sister named Margie Faires, living about twenty miles away in Huntersville, whom she felt sure would like to attend as well. Mamie Cole hesitated at first because of her age, but when I promised to drive her into the site on the ATV, she happily agreed. Dan Rankin accepted. He was a distant cousin directly descended from James C. Rankin, whose father had taken him to see the tree as a young boy in the late 1950s. Finally, I pitched the story to Joe DePriest, local newspaper columnist for *The Charlotte Observer*, and he was interested. Over the next several weeks, clearing the dirt driveway and cutting paths around the old Rankin home site prepared the place for our group's reunion visit.

Saturday, October 19, was a beautiful fall day. Sharon Wilson had the conservancy's ATV at the ready. Another distant cousin, Haywood Rankin, who started the land trust movement in Gaston County, joined Wilson. Picking up Mamie Cole at her home, we met the rest of the group at the bottom of my driveway at 10:00 am. There were twelve of us in all, including Wilson and Haywood Rankin who were already waiting at the road entrance. Nell Crouse came with her friend Ed Morton and brought her son Steve Crouse and daughter Debra Payseur. Margie Faires came with her daughter Elaine Faires and grandson Adam Gant. Dan Rankin attended too.

When we arrived at the site, I asked Cole, Crouse, and Faires to tell me independently and without consulting each other once we got to the old house site where they thought the great tree originally stood. Nell Crouse cleverly observed that determining if my stump hole really was the spot of the Rankin Oak should be easy: if so, then concrete from the tree repair would be scattered around the tree base. Once there, Faires pointed exactly to the spot where I found my stump hole. Crouse was off by only a few yards. Cole was unsure. We carefully moved closer to the spot through a tangle of trees and vines. There as predicted were scattered chunks of concrete around the perimeter of the stump's ground cavity. *This was what remained of the Rankin Oak.* I had been right about its location (35*20'681" N, 81*03'261" W).

We spent the next hour meandering around the site as the ladies remembered their home. The cleared paths could not contain them. Soon we were off trail exploring the farther reaches of the place. Mamie Cole grabbed my arm and off we went to discover old outbuildings, a few of them badly decayed but still standing. Our foray provided an unanticipated, exciting find. Another southern red oak over four feet in diameter at breast height and seventy-five feet tall stood about thirty yards southwest of the house site. Covered with fungus on half of the lower trunk, the massive tree did not look particularly healthy. But it was alive and probably a close relative of the Rankin Oak.

The visit to the old homeplace felt strangely beyond time. So many years came back to life in the memories of Cole, Crouse, and Faires. What year was it really? 1930? 1945? 2012? All of the above? Those who attended the Rankin Oak reunion left the place—some for perhaps the last time—and drove over to our home for lunch. There we read Joe DePriest's article, published that morning under the headline, "Group to gather for reunion honoring a long-gone tree." Then we ate a meal together that my wife prepared. She also copied pictures on her photo scanner that Crouse and Faires had brought of the old home and part of the great tree's base. The whole day was happy and satisfying. That feeling lingered with my wife and me for several days afterwards.

Because of the citation in *Trees of the Southeastern States*, the Rankin Oak will never be completely forgotten. However, as important as its official history may be, more significant were the rich, meaningful relationships that developed between the great tree and at least four generations of inhabitants. Ralph and Estelle Rankin, Rome and Mamie Allison, and Nell and Margie Huffstetler felt genuine affection for and sympathy with the Rankin Oak and enjoyed being in its presence. E. O. Wilson, renowned American biologist, speculates that all humans share an instinctive affection for all living creatures, called *biophilia*. Howard Thurman, one of America's great twentieth century spiritual leaders and mystics, cherished his own intimate relationship with a special oak tree that grew in his front yard as a child in Daytona, Florida. Thurman's bond with his special tree had mystical and transcendent qualities.

In reflecting on how often the Allison and Huffstetler children played next to the Rankin Oak, many of us will recall our own childhoods and how much we enjoyed our favorite trees. Child's play under or in a tree has always been highly imaginative and creative. According to Thurman, great trees like the Rankin Oak not only bring us into relationship with other living creatures; they also connect us to a Greater Mystery that unites and sustains all creation.

The people who knew the Rankin Oak were joined through its great age to distant times past. The tree itself was a witness to the Catawba nation, Anglo-American pioneers, enslaved African Americans, Civil War veterans, and twentieth century tenant farming families. The great hardwood tree influenced and heartened those who dwelled with it and continues to connect a small fellowship of friends and relatives—a few living, more dead—to a particular place and past. The giant tree's size, age, and majesty made it a spectacular living being, impressing all who saw it, fostering companionship across species, and inspiring awe and wonder. Its history symbolizes how great trees enrich our lives and bind us more fully to the special places in creation we call home.

See William Chambers Coker and Henry Roland Totten, *Trees of the Southeastern States: Including Virginia, North Carolina, South Carolina, Tennessee, Georgia, and Northern Florida*, 2nd ed. (Chapel Hill: University of North Carolina Press, 1937). This essay first appeared in a longer version in my *Margins of a Greater Wildness: Nature Essays about Stanley Creek and Beyond* (Mt. Holly, NC: Willow Hill Press, 2014), 31–53.

5

Last of the Catawba Dogs

All around the globe, domesticated dogs occasionally go wild and band together in packs. This phenomenon of reverting to wildness has been a constant feature in the history of our domesticated canines. Growing up in Piedmont North Carolina in the 1960s, we called these dogs "strays." There was nothing mysterious or remarkable about stray dogs—or so we thought. They were just groups of our pets and working dogs that abandoned domestication to resume an unfettered, unleashed way of life. They were common then, and they are common now.

Over the last thirty-five years, however, wild dog populations have been discovered in the Southeast that challenge our original thinking and raise the possibility of more ancient dogs surviving in our midst. These dogs have been given various names: Carolina Dogs, Indian Dogs, Dixie Dingoes, and American Dingoes. Their different names reflect controversial, uncertain origins. Before Thanksgiving 2011, I never dreamed that these wild dogs lived in Gaston County. Now I believe they do.

The first wild dogs I ever saw were about 150 miles southeast of Gaston County in the South Carolina Lowcountry. In the early 1970s, we bird hunted on land that my father and uncle leased near the Pocotaligo Swamp, an area about seven miles east of Manning, South Carolina. Our hunting party was several hundred yards from the big low-country swamp when a small pack of wild dogs crossed the sandy road in front of us and disappeared quickly into the oak scrub. On another occasion, while hunting in a canebrake on the swamp's edge, our hunting guide Henry Hilton warned me to be prepared to defend myself in case of a wild dog attack. But the dogs never materialized. Toward the end of our hunt club's existence, Hilton found a den of wild puppies and raised one as a pet. During our fifteen years of hunting near the swamp at the Quail Roost Hunt Club, the wild dogs were an eerie presence, seldom seen but lurking near the swamp and alive in our imaginations. Hilton, who lived near the swamp, spoke of them with easy familiarity. It was as if they had been there forever. *Maybe they had.*

Although wild dogs were scattered throughout South Carolina and Georgia's swamps and river bottoms during the 1960s and 1970s, knowledge of them was strictly local. Our group of Manning hunters was typical: we knew only about the Pocotaligo Swamp dogs and no others. Presumably, local inhabitants in other places were similarly aware of just their resident wild dogs. Perhaps a few state-level wildlife biologists possessed a broad enough perspective to realize that wild dog populations were more widespread. But certainly the general public was ignorant of their existence. Coincidentally, at almost the same time that I encountered wild dogs near Manning, field ecologist Dr. I. Lehr Brisbin Jr. began his pioneering research at the Savannah River Ecology Laboratory near Aiken, South Carolina. His work would lead to public recognition of Southeastern wild dogs and to the establishment of the Carolina Dog breed. But that conclusion remained more than a decade away.

Carolina Dogs are medium-sized, slim, muscular dogs, weighing from thirty-five to sixty pounds. Depending on whom you ask, they resemble a small, light-red German shepherd with a shorter coat or even a light-colored Basenji. But the closest lookalike of all is the Australian Dingo, and Carolina Dogs are often called the American Dingo because of the remarkable resemblance. Two distinguishing features are the pointed ears and the fishhook tail. In the wild, they hunt in packs and are classified as sight hounds. Even when domesticated, Carolina Dogs are extremely alert and cautious within their environment. They seem to retain a wild animal's constant vigilance and imminent sense of danger.

There are three main theories of Carolina Dog origin. The first argues that Carolina Dogs are descended from aboriginal dogs that crossed the Bering Land Bridge and thus were related to other primitive dogs of Asia and Oceania. A second origin theory contends that these canines represent a separate population derived from an independent process of North American domestication. Accordingly, in a way similar to dog domestication on other continents, 14,000 to more than 30,000 years ago, some North American wolves began to be attracted to the waste and scraps around early human settlements. Native Americans adopted and tamed the most docile of these wild canines and created North American dogs. So, in this theory, Carolina Dogs are neither of Asian nor European lineages. They are true American dogs. Finally, a third origin theory maintains Carolina Dogs are simply feral canines descended from European breeds of domesticated dogs that, like other feral animals, have evolved backwards after many generations in the wild to a more basic "dog" body type. According to this view, any pack of strays, no matter how genetically diverse and confused, will become Carolina Dogs after enough generations in the wild. Why? Because the Carolina Dog's basic form and body type provide distinct survival advantages in a wild environment. This, so the argument goes, is why "pariah dogs"—a class of feral dogs living around the world on the fringe of civilization, often near garbage dumps—resemble each other and Carolina Dogs. They all evolved back to the fittest type.

There is a great deal at stake in which of these theories is correct. If it is the latter, then Carolina Dogs are just highly evolved strays. They may have regained wild qualities, but they certainly are not an endangered species. Their existence is secure whenever and wherever strays go feral and resume their basic body type after enough generations of wild breeding. However, if these wild dogs are American Dingoes or an independent American wild dog, then we are dealing with a species that is ancient and has continuously occupied an environment originally shared with Native Americans. In that case the breed is not only a rare survival, needing our protection to avoid extinction, but a living link with our Native American past. Which of these theories is correct? Could more than one theory be correct? Could Carolina Dogs conceivably come from either two or all three of these theoretical dog populations that have interbred? Can genetic testing on Carolina Dogs reveal which of these theories or some combination of them is correct? The answer is *not yet*. DNA analysis of Carolina Dogs remains presently inconclusive, and the debate about Carolina Dog origins agitates and swirls. While we wait on the science, wild Carolina Dogs still prowl swamps and rivers, facing greater pressure as humans encroach and coyotes invade their territory and interbreed.

My interest in Carolina Dogs might have remained limited to the previous experiences on the Pocotaligo Swamp and reading about their emergence as a new breed if not for my visit during my 2011 Thanksgiving vacation to Winchester's Antique Shop on the Hickory Grove Road in the Springwood section, Gaston County. Jack Winchester, the owner, introduced me to his female dog Dinga, a gorgeous, blue-eyed Carolina Dog. Aware of the natural history of Carolina Dogs from my own reading, I asked Winchester if Dinga came from South Carolina or Georgia. Frankly, I was incredulous when he responded no and told me he caught Dinga about two years earlier from the wild on the South Fork River near Hardin in north-central Gaston County. Winchester said that he became fascinated with Carolina Dogs well before he found Dinga and learned all he could about them. On the particular day of Dinga's capture, he and a friend hauled a load of scrap metal from Lincolnton and took a back road at High Shoals toward Hardin. Just below the shoals, a light-red dog with stunning blue eyes ran across the road, and Winchester pulled over to investigate. Right away, Winchester thought he was seeing a Carolina Dog, although he had never heard of one outside South Carolina and Georgia. When questioned about this, he explains that you must believe Carolina Dogs exist before you can see one. According to him, finding a Carolina Dog is like spotting a classic, vintage Edsel automobile. If you are unfamiliar with Edsels, you will not see one. But once you own an Edsel, as rare as they are, you begin to notice others infrequently passing you in traffic. In the same way, Winchester feels that his interest in Carolina Dogs prepared him to recognize Dinga when she ran across the road in front of him.

Catching Dinga that day involved an element of pure luck. When the young female ran toward the river to escape, she accidentally trapped herself in a strand of chicken wire. There Winchester finally got a rope around her as she spun and howled like a banshee, but even so never tried to bite him. When Winchester arrived home with his wild dog, wife Penny Winchester thought the dog was rabid and her husband crazy. Knowing that Lehr Brisbin called his wild dogs American Dingoes, Winchester feminized her name to Dinga. With Dinga in a backyard pen, he used food scraps over the next few weeks to gradually gain her trust. Soon the female dog became totally attached to her new master, and Jack Winchester and Dinga became inseparable.

Though hard to believe, Winchester's story was full of convincing details and had the ring of truth. Could there really be wild Carolina Dogs in Gaston County, North Carolina, less than fifteen miles from Charlotte and inside the thirty-third largest metropolitan region in the nation? Thus began my intensive, exciting search for local Carolina Dogs, leading to an even greater interest in the breed. At first, it was a Google search that revealed that Carolina Dogs were turning up outside South Carolina and Georgia in other remote river bottoms and Southeastern wildernesses. If this was so, then Dinga's discovery fit a growing pattern, although the South Fork hardly seemed especially wild.

What happened next still amazes me. During the second week of December 2011, I drove home from Lincolnton down US Highway 321 late Saturday morning after doing some family history research in the library there. After crossing the bridge over the South Fork River, I spotted a cream-colored dog eating a deer carcass on the highway shoulder. At first skeptical about what I thought I saw, I decided to turn around, circle back on the divided highway, and see if the dog was still there. Veering off the nearest exit to head back, I was amazed to see that the highway sign indicated that this was the Hardin exit—*I was near where Jack Winchester found Dinga.* Because US 321 is a divided highway, it took several minutes to exit, reverse north to the previous exit, turn around again, and retrace my route across the river. Would the dog be gone? As I crossed the South Fork for the second time, I looked expectantly. *The dog was still there gnawing on the deer.* I got out of the car and moved toward it, stopping not more than twenty yards away. Our eyes locked only for an instant before the frightened creature scrambled up the embankment as fast as possible to escape me. There was no doubt about it: I had just stared into a wild dog's eyes. Lighter in color than most Carolina Dogs and somewhat emaciated, the dog had tucked its tail between its legs. I could not tell its sex or if its small ears were pointed (like a Carolina Dog's) or pendant. But it generally looked similar to the breed. And there was no doubt that it was wild. Dinga was neither the only nor the last wild dog on the South Fork near Hardin. I had seen another one up close.

Encountering this wild dog seemed so weird and unexpected that it left me wondering: was I meant to find wild Carolina Dogs on the South Fork? I felt a tremendous urge to discover more and to catch one as a mate for Dinga. My wife was bemused and maintained that I had become obsessed with Carolina Dogs. Cryptozoology is the term used for people who search for animals whose existence is unproven (e.g., the Loch Ness Monster). Even I joked that my search for Carolina Dogs was like looking for Bigfoot or an ivory-billed woodpecker. With the advantage of hindsight, I realize that my search for Carolina Dogs was part of a lifelong attraction to wildness, wonder, and mystery.

Jack Winchester shared my excitement over the discovery of another wild dog, and he was enthusiastic too about the prospect of captive breeding South Fork wild dogs, just as Lehr Brisbin and others had done in South Carolina. Winchester himself hunted for other South Fork wild dogs after catching Dinga, but with no success, and he ultimately abandoned the possibility of finding more. Instead, he bred Dinga to one of Dr. Don Anderson's wild-caught Carolina Dogs from his wild dog preserve on Lynches River near Bishopville, South Carolina. The two offspring, one male and one female, had a motley-colored coat like their father rather than Dinga's beautiful light red color.

Over the Christmas holiday, I had time off from school duties to look for wild dogs. First, I explored the South Fork River near High Shoals and Hardin in my truck, occasionally stopping to quiz local residents about strays and wild dogs. Upon closer inspection, the stretch of river from the Laboratory community in Lincoln County down through High Shoals and Hardin to Spencer Mountain in Gaston County was much wilder and undeveloped than I previously realized. Also, there were at least two important features relevant to wild dogs: one historical and one contemporary. A Native American village had been situated at present-day Hardin and remained inhabited until the 1500s. These people were the ancestors of the Catawba tribe. Dogs had certainly populated the river at one time in its history, and, conceivably, surviving wild dogs might be descended from these original native dogs. Could Dinga be one of the last of the Catawba Dogs? Second, the Gaston County Landfill on Philadelphia Church Road was close to the South Fork, and feral dogs love garbage dumps.

With one exception, the feedback from my first day's interviews was inconclusive and even discouraging. When I stopped at the High Shoals Volunteer Fire Department, two young firemen knew nothing. But they did suggest I return the next day to speak to a woman who they thought might know more. John Clark, who lives on Spring Road in Hardin, did claim that wild dogs had always been present in the area and that a male with a cropped tail lived on the back of his property. Clark's testimony was the most promising of the day.

The second day was different. When I returned to the High Shoals Volunteer Fire Department, the local woman did not show up. But I found that Fire Chief Brian Cash had heard about my inquiry of the previous day, and he had a story to tell—a recent one, full of convincing details. Only about a week earlier, he and his grandson were preparing to go deer hunting in the front yard of his house on Dayton Road about a half-mile from the shoals. Suddenly, they looked up and saw two wild dogs chasing a deer from the woods across the street and into Cash's front yard. For a moment, Cash thought he might have to shoot in self-defense as the dogs closed to within ten yards. But at the last second, the dogs veered and fled. Cash described them as looking "half yellow lab and half coyote"—a pretty apt description of a Carolina Dog. The fire chief had spotted the wild dogs less than 500 yards from where Dinga was caught and about a half a mile from the bridge over the South Fork River on US Highway 321. These were different dogs than the one I had seen near the Hwy 321 Bridge, and presumably they were still at large near High Shoals.

Excited by Cash's story, I resumed my search. Trying to think like a wild dog, I headed several miles away to the Gaston County Landfill. Several landfill employees indicated that Barry Cloninger, a veteran employee, was the resident expert. But Cloninger had ridden to the other side of the landfill and was unavailable. When I returned several days later, what Cloninger told me only added to my growing conviction that there were still Carolina Dogs on the South Fork. According to him, until about 2001, "Red Dog," an alpha male wild dog, and his pack of ten to twelve dogs frequented the landfill. Cloninger was able to accurately date the time because he remembered that it was when county workers lined the landfill with clay. Cloninger's description of Red Dog and his pack sounded like Carolina Dogs, although he distinctly remembered that Red Dog's ears were semi-pricked instead of standing completely erect to breed standard. Red Dog and his pack were so familiar with landfill workers that the pack leader would look up when they called his name. One time they even doused his mangy back with motor oil to help it heal, which it did. But Red Dog and his pack would not let anyone touch them.

Being alone with the landfill pack could be frightening. One late afternoon, Cloninger drove by himself to the back of the property. When he got out to walk into the field, he suddenly realized that the pack had surrounded him, and he quickly retreated to the safety of his vehicle. Several years later, Red Dog and his pack disappeared from the landfill, and Cloninger honestly did not know what happened to them. I asked if county officials had intentionally eliminated the pack, and he said no. But I couldn't help wondering if

Gaston County Animal Control had caught and euthanized them. Probably other local residents spotted them, became fearful, and called the dogcatcher. After all, Animal Control was supposed to catch strays.

After several days of investigation, I was more and more convinced that Carolina Dogs were still living on the South Fork River between Laboratory and Spencer Mountain. First and foremost, there was Dinga, a blue-eyed Carolina Dog captured just below the High Shoals. Second, I saw the wild dog at the US Hwy 321 Bridge, but its appearance was somewhat indistinct. Now I learned that High Shoals Fire Chief Cash had spotted two wild dogs fitting the description of Carolina Dogs. And Barry Cloninger described a pack of dingo-like wild dogs that had occupied the county landfill not long ago.

Another chance encounter over the holiday fit the emerging pattern of evidence. While driving home through Stanley one afternoon, I saw a woman walking what looked like a four- or five-year-old overweight Carolina Dog. Three months earlier, I would have driven past the dog without a second thought, but now, like Jack Winchester, I believed in the existence of local Carolina Dogs. So I stopped to ask the friendly stranger, and she told me her story. She found the female dog as a dirty, abandoned, healthy puppy—without a collar—on the Spencer Mountain Road midway between the South Fork River Bridge and Hickory Grove Road, or about 500 yards from the lower end of the territory where I found evidence of wild dogs. She assumed that its owner dumped it, which was certainly possible or even probable. But given my recent interviews, I also wondered if it could have been wild originally.

Other evidence gathered over Christmas break was less

conclusive. Two telephone calls made to longtime South Fork farmers yielded no support for Carolina Dogs. My friend Frederick Carpenter, living on an old family farm near Pasour Mountain near the Laboratory community, had never seen a wild dog. Nor had his neighbors whom he quizzed. Frederick was an avid fox hunter and seasoned outdoorsman who knew his natural surroundings well. Similarly, Bill Rhyne, another older farmer whose family lived for many generations at Sandcastle Farm just west of Hoyle's Bridge on the South Fork, had once seen three wild dogs, but none looked like a Carolina Dog.

Was I deceiving myself about Carolina Dogs on the South Fork River? Could wild dogs really be living in the river bottom and many local inhabitants not realize it? Why had Bill Rhyne and Frederick Carpenter, who spent their whole lives in the woods close to the river, never seen a Carolina Dog? For a historian, credible evidence is paramount. Dinga was real. But the Stanley dog could be an abandoned pet. The wild dog at the Hwy 321 Bridge was lighter in color than most Carolina Dogs and may have been a stray. In the cases of Brian Cash and Barry Cloninger, I was depending on two eyewitness accounts, but both seemed reliable. At what point, I asked myself, was I willing to announce my discovery that Carolina Dogs survived on the South Fork? The answer was *not yet*.

Although I shared my growing conviction with close friends and family, I wanted more indisputable proof: either to capture a wild Carolina Dog or to photograph one using a new motion-sensing wildlife camera. Capturing a male was especially desirable since Jack Winchester and I could breed it to Dinga and have pure South Fork River Dogs. But I had absolutely no experience trapping wild animals and great doubts about my ability to do so. After some consideration and consultation with my tech-savvy wife, I decided a wildlife camera was more practical.

Fortunately, a local landowner, known through our mutual involvement with the Catawba Lands Conservancy, owned a wooded tract about a half mile from the shoals and across the road from Brian Cash's house. When I called for permission to put my wildlife camera on his property, he gladly consented. I also asked whether he had ever seen any Carolina Dogs. At first, he said that in all his years of trapping on the river, he had not. But then, on second thought, he remembered once taking a picture of two nearby dogs that might have been wild. With his consent, I installed a motion-activated camera on his property in the hope that I would capture an image of a Carolina Dog. During the next six weeks, I felt no need to communicate with the property owner, a decision I later greatly regretted.

My photography project was both exciting and enjoyable. The camera was tied around a tree about fifty yards into the woods. The school dining hall saved buckets of food waste that I used as bait. Usually each Saturday morning, I made the twenty-minute ride to the site, replenished the bait, and switched out the camera chip with a new one. Sometimes there was a frustrating technical glitch that wasted an entire week: usually a dead battery. But often the camera did its job. Then I drove home and let my wife load the chip into our laptop for viewing, each time hoping that a Carolina Dog would be revealed. The camera captured abundant wildlife images: coyotes, domestic dogs, cats, deer, opossums, vultures, and lots of raccoons, *but no Carolina Dogs*.

After about six weeks of failing to photograph a

Carolina Dog, it was time to call the property owner, give him an update, and ask about relocating my camera closer to the river. The ensuing conversation was a bombshell. He told me that right after we last spoke, to his utter shock and surprise, three wild dogs began regularly raiding his garbage cans. He tried to call me but failed in part because I had a new cell phone number. An experienced trapper, the landowner live-caught two of the wild dogs, but the third was extremely wary and evaded him. The two captured dogs were both males about a year old and closely fit the description of a Carolina Dog with some gray hair in their coats. While both were handsome, one was particularly healthy and vigorous and the other more beat up. The third dog was a thin male with a lighter coat.

The trapper turned the two dogs over to Gaston County Animal Control, and presumably they were put down. When I asked Animal Control what happened to these two dogs' records, they produced none. Although there is absolutely no way to be certain, I believe the two captured dogs were the ones that chased the deer into Chief Cash's yard, and the lighter dog—probably still free today—was the one I spotted at the Hwy 321 Bridge. If so, they formed a small pack of three wild dogs. It will always be a terrible disappointment that Jack Winchester and I did not have a chance to save those two wild dogs. I believe they were wild Carolina Dogs—maybe like Dinga, some of the last of their kind.

The South Fork of the Catawba River is wilder, richer, and more mysterious now that we know a small population of wild dogs lives there. The location of the Gaston County Landfill on the river near Hardin probably attracts wild dogs from up and down the river corridor, just as it did Red Dog's pack. These dogs may be a living link to the prehistoric dogs that lived in the Native American village near Hardin, or the South Fork River may be wild enough to have naturally selected a new generation of pariah dogs descended from formerly domesticated strays. But whatever their origins, Carolina Dogs are present on the South Fork in Gaston County today. Believe it or not.

This essay first appeared in a longer version in my *Margins of a Greater Wildness*, 106–22. For Carolina Dog origins see Jane Rittenhouse Gunnell, *Carolina Dogs: The American Dingos* (Aiken, SC: Howell Printing, 2004), 4; B.F. Koop, M. Burbridge, A. Byun, U. Rink, and S. J. Crockford, "Ancient DNA Evidence of a Separate Origin for North American Indigenous Dogs," in Susan J. Crockford, ed., *Dogs through Time: An Archaeological Perspective* (Oxford: British Archaeology Reports, 2008), 271–85; and Jack Hitt, "DNA Backs Lore on Pre-Columbian Dogs," *New York Times*, July 15, 2013.

6

The Negro War

By Frank Bisaner Rankin
(Lincoln County's False Enslaved Insurrection
Panic after Nat Turner's Rebellion)

Note: For the original manuscript by my grandfather written in 1897, see Frank Bisaner Rankin, "Negro War," Rankin Family Papers, Manuscript Collection, J. Murrey Atkins Library Special Collections, UNC Charlotte. My grandfather uses dated or racially insensitive, offensive terms to refer to Black people throughout his account.

About the year 1830, Colonel John Hoke of Lincolnton, North Carolina, was in command of the [militia] regiment in Lincoln County, which then embraced the present counties of Catawba, Lincoln, Gaston, and Cleveland. Several weeks after the spring review, a rumor was started to the effect that the Negro slaves were planning a sudden revolt. All kinds of reports were rife concerning their plots. This news spread like wildfire, and in forty-eight hours from the time the alarm started, the militia was under arms and the whole county aroused.

The negroes, as many as were suspected, were confined in strong cabins under strong guards who had instructions to burn the prisons at the first attempt to escape. Meanwhile, the [White] wives and children were collected at the strongest houses in the community. These houses were also under guard. It was early in April and the weather was rather cold. At Lincolnton the women and children had collected in the courthouse. The good dames bringing provisions of all kinds, but chiefly coffee. My father relates that all of the flat railing around the bar was lined with coffee pots of all descriptions. The militia slept on their arms that night, ready at a minute's call to go to the scene of action, wherever that was. Scouts traversed the country in every direction.

Early the next morning, a horseman dashed into town, his horse covered with foam. He reported the enemy to be at Fulinwider's forge seven miles northwest of L[incolnton]; that they had, under the leadership of Big Jim, hammer-man at the forge, burned Andrew Fulinwider's house and were now moving toward town. Immediately the alarm sounded, the men fell into line, and with Col. Hoke in command, the column headed for the seat of hostilities. The regiment was armed with every conceivable kind of weapons from muskets and pitchforks to clubs and scythes. There were all kinds of horse, from the blooded gray of Col. Hoke and the high headed stallion of Capt. Rankin to Nick Goslin's claybank filly, which he rode bareback, armed with a pitch-fork and wearing two huge spurs on his naked feet. An hour's hard riding brought the troops to the vicinity of the reported outrage.

The valley in which Mr. Fulinwider's factory was situated is one of pleasing aspect. The hills rise in smooth, grassy slopes on either side. There is a varying width of lowland between them checked with ditches through which a small river, the South Fork of the Catawba, runs. Beside this river a road goes, leading up to the furnace. Above these works, the hills seem to come almost together, forming a narrow gorge through which the river rushes. The water power here is used to turn machinery of the forge while the bold hills on the sides furnish a supply of ore seemingly inexhaustible.

Col. Hoke led his men up the road. When within a half-mile of the iron factory, everyone was startled by an unearthly sound that came from the neighborhood of the ware-house just below the main building. It seemed that twenty trip-hammers and [an] artillery fight were all turned loose at once. Some of the men were thoroughly frightened; many wanted to go back. The commander called a halt and held a council of war. It was decided to *separate* the force and surround the place. Accordingly, Capt. Rich'd Rankin was ordered to take one half the forces, cross the river at a nearby ford, and ascend on the other side; while Col. Hoke himself led the rest up the eastern side. They met in opposition and soon formed a circle around the supposed enemy.

The sound from the store-house continued. As no enemy yet appeared, the circle moved forward, closing in as it grew smaller. A solid line was formed in a short time, extending around the iron house. No enemy yet appeared; the ware-house was closed and locked from the outside. Could they be preparing for a rally, and the lock [be] simply a blind? At length, several men advanced and hailed the house; no answer. A beam was procured, the door broken, and lo! What did they find? Only "a n-gg-r and a mule." Mr. Fulinwider had heard of the trouble and taken his negroes to a neighboring farm. A crowd passing saw this negro riding past and, thinking him a negro scout, they caught and imprisoned both mule and negro. The restless mule explained the horrible noise.

Pushing on to the Andrew Fulinwider's before mentioned, Col. Hoke found the family of that gentleman alive and able to get him an excellent dinner, which he heartily enjoyed after the excitement of the morning. After the troops had been refreshed from the storehouses of the neighborhood and the scouts had returned reporting no signs of insurrection anywhere, they slowly began to disband. By night[,] all but a few daring spirits were at home. Col. Hoke marched back to town and went to the jail where the negroes were confined. He ordered the jailer to open the doors, and when the darkies were all in the courtyard, Col. Hoke in his peculiarly shrill voice shouted, "I'll give you five minutes to get home. If anyone is caught out after that he will be shot." The effect was electrical. All that could be seen were hats and feet. In two minutes not a son of Ham was visible.

A party of picked men was dispatched to capture Big Jim. They arrived at his shanty a little after dark. There was no light, and they thought that their prey had fled. However, they advanced cautiously and pushed the door open. There stretched upon his bed with arms extended lay the giant frame of the supposed leader, while the air was vibrating from the shock caused by his snoring. They did not disturb his rest but went away convinced that the alarm was false. Thus was ended the "n-gg-r war."

In 1897, as a nineteen-year-old college student, Frank Bisaner Rankin wrote the paper reproduced above on the topic of "The Negro War" in Lincoln County, North Carolina. His only source was his ninety-three-year-old father, Colonel Richard Rankin, who was himself a participant and eyewitness to the long distant events about which his son wrote. Rankin family members farmed in east-central Lincoln County for several generations and also served as prominent local public officials, and they continued to do so after 1846 when their property was incorporated into newly formed Gaston County. Richard Rankin was able to recall and relate the events of the false enslaved-insurrection panic that took place sixty-six years prior to his nineteen-year-old son's description of it because the colonel was seventy-four years old when his much younger third wife Delia Bisaner Rankin gave birth to their son Frank Bisaner Rankin.

The episode that Colonel Rankin described was an aftermath of the Nat Turner Rebellion, the American South's greatest enslaved insurrection, which took place in Southampton County, Virginia, in August 1831. The related Lincoln County panic happened shortly afterwards in the last week of September or the first week of October 1831. Although Richard Rankin claimed he served as a militia captain in the panic, he actually was a young, regular Lincoln County militia member. This all took place long before he rose to command Gaston County's militia and obtained the rank of colonel after the new county's formation.

Nat Turner's Rebellion terrified White people throughout Virginia and North Carolina and reverberated all the way to Lincoln County. The uprising killed from fifty-five to sixty-five Whites—the highest number of fatalities for any such revolt in the American South. The rebellion was crushed in only a few days, although Turner remained at large in hiding for more than two months before being caught and put to death. The State of Virginia executed fifty-six enslaved persons convicted of being part of the revolt. Mobs and militias killed at least another 100 and probably more than 200 Blacks.

In North Carolina, Turner's Rebellion generated widespread panic and fear of homegrown enslaved uprisings. In late September, Whites in the southeastern counties of New Hanover, Duplin, Sampson, Wayne, and Lenoir believed that they had uncovered a related rebellion before it was hatched. A small number of reputed enslaved ringleaders were brought to trial and executed. There were also documented fears in Northampton County on the Virginia border, Cumberland and Montgomery counties in the Sandhills, and as far west as Rutherford and Burke counties in the Appalachian Foothills. In Burke, a group of enslaved workers employed in gold mining were suspected of plotting insurrection. Although the details surrounding the Burke County gold-mining insurrection fears are sparse, at least superficially, that episode bears some resemblance to those in Lincoln County that also involved enslaved industrial laborers. Particularly, in the last week of September and the first week of October, the suspicions appear to have spread to various places in the western part of the state and climaxed. On October 5, *The Charlotte Journal* described "the excitement and alarm which has prevailed so extensively for the last few days."

Although the Charlotte newspaper indicated local fears, no contemporary account specifically mentioned anything about an enslaved insurrection scare in nearby Lincoln County. As a well-established farmer and militia member who lived in the east-central part of the county as the panic unfolded, Richard Rankin experienced the crisis firsthand. His memories formed the basis of his son Frank Rankin's eleven-hundred-word account. As a writer and historical researcher, Frank Rankin probably had no idea that he was preserving a rare account of the aftershocks of Turner's

Rebellion, which threw Lincoln County into brief social and military chaos. His narrative makes clear how the White establishment panicked in reaction to false rumors that they were under attack by their own enslaved people. It also demonstrates how antebellum Lincoln County's enslaved labor system fostered a prevailing environment of fear for both Whites and Blacks, and life-threatening injustice for enslaved people of color.

As the lone primary source some sixty-plus years after the events of Lincoln County's panic, how reliable was Richard Rankin's testimony? And how accurate was Frank Rankin's understanding and interpretation of his father's story? The answers to those two questions merit further explanation and qualification. In several instances where the details of the story can be checked, there are minor mistakes. The events are described as happening "about the year 1830" and "early in April." So the year 1831 is certainly "about" right, but the season is wrong. Events transpired sometime between the last week in September and the first week in October 1831. There is at least one partial mistake of identity. The owner of the High Shoals Iron Factory, scene of much of the action, was identified as Andrew Fulinwider when actually he was Jacob Fulenwider. So the first name was wrong, and the surname, though a variant spelling, was correct. Jacob Fulenwider's father-in-law was the highly successful local merchant Andrew Hoyle. The close association between the father and son-in-law may have caused a transposition of the first name.

There is also at least one mistake of geographical location. The High Shoals Iron Factory was located not "seven miles northwest of" Lincolnton but instead seven miles southeast. Perhaps this error can be explained as a simple confusion of reference points. The author may have been thinking of Lincolnton's position relative to High Shoals, instead of vice versa. All these minor errors make sense given the long passage of time, faulty memory involving details, and possible miscommunication between the father/narrator and son/writer.

The biggest misrepresentation of all, however, was the exaggerated rank that "Capt. Rich'd Rankin" assigned himself in the action. Richard Rankin was in his late twenties at the time of Nat Turner's Rebellion, owned eleven enslaved people, and was on his way up in a political career that would see him become a leader in the creation of Gaston County (1846), Gaston County militia commander, Gaston County general assembly representative, and Gaston County commission chairman. He aspired to higher militia rank by the date of the "Negro War." On December 27, 1829, Rankin inscribed his copy of a book purchased: William Duane, *A Military Dictionary, or Explanation of the Several Systems of Discipline of Different Kinds of Troops, Infantry, Artillery, and Cavalry; The Principles of Fortifications, and All the Modern Improvements in the Science of Tactics* (Philadelphia: the author, 1819). So he was already studying military science that would help him gain later promotions. But Rankin was not yet a captain, despite what he later told his son. In 1830, a year before the Negro War, he is identified in the Federal Census as just plain "Richard Rankin," while other Lincoln County militia officers listed in the census have their ranks prefixed to their names, including many captains. There is no evidence that Rankin was made captain during the interim. In recollecting the events of sixty-plus years earlier, Richard Rankin gave himself a premature promotion.

Beyond his false promotion, it also is questionable whether Richard Rankin commanded half the troop in the maneuver to surround the High Shoals Iron Factory as described in the story. Colonel Hoke had other, more experienced captains present to put in charge. At the same time, however, Rankin's subsequent militia career saw him rise to commander of the Gaston County militia. And he had already begun studying military tactics in Duane's *Military Dictionary.* So perhaps Colonel Hoke recognized that the youthful Rankin possessed special military knowledge and a growing sense of command. Maybe Hoke really did pick Rankin to help lead the assault.

Regardless of whether Richard Rankin aggrandized his role in the assault on the iron factory, he was definitely an eyewitness and active participant in these events, and he surely remembered the main contours of what happened clearly and vividly. Family tradition maintains that Rankin remained completely lucid and active nearly until his death in 1899. Despite the list of minor inaccuracies and the major exaggeration of Richard Rankin's rank, the story's details otherwise match the existing historical record.

Not only is Frank Rankin's account for the most part historically correct, but it has an unusual ring of truth. This is not a story that a participant was likely to have fabricated. The behavior of the White militia—confused, hesitant, and mistaken—contradicts the image that the White establishment hoped to project. The episode is also one that a participant would likely never forget. Some of the images are especially compelling. For instance, the description of the Lincolnton ladies retreating to the courthouse for safety with all manner of provisions and then lining the courthouse railing with all their coffee pots. Or the captive mule. Or

Colonel Hoke's shrill warning to the released enslaved Blacks in Lincolnton. Or Big Jim sleeping and snoring soundly inside his house. Making up such vivid, specific events seems impossible. Even with the long time lapse between the panic and when Frank Rankin wrote about it, this is certainly a mainly reliable account from an eyewitness source of an important and revealing chapter of local and state history. Other than an Episcopal minister's description of the Wilmington insurrection alarm in southeastern North Carolina (recorded in his diary as the events unfolded), Rankin's account may be the most complete historical record of the particulars of a local panic in North Carolina. It suggests the nature of the broader White alarm and the ensuing victimization of enslaved persons in other places across the state.

Besides militia man Richard Rankin, three other figures were in the forefront of the action. Two of them were politically prominent. Colonel John Hoke, commander of the Lincoln militia, was one of the county's most distinguished merchants and earliest textile manufacturers. His handsome antebellum mansion still sits on a beautiful hillside above the South Fork River in the community of Laboratory, about three miles north of the former site of the High Shoals Iron Factory. Jacob Fulenwider (misidentified as Andrew Fulinwider) succeeded his father as one of the most successful iron manufacturers in the region, and the site of his famous manufacturing plant at High Shoals is well described in the text. The third person, Big Jim, enslaved laborer and hammer-man, is previously unknown to history. With him comes a glimpse of an enslaved industrial laborer whose position as hammer-man was one of the most highly skilled and critical to the iron-making process. An unusually big, strong man, Big Jim's high standing in the enslaved community is further implied by the immediate suspicion that he was the leader of the insurrection. With his "giant frame," he must have been an imposing figure.

While no other contemporary description of Lincoln's enslaved uprising panic survives, the county court minutes of the October 1831 session do reflect the charged atmosphere. The minutes make no specific mention of the local disturbance—which is not surprising given the embarrassing nature of the whole affair for the White establishment—but county leaders did take actions that reflected the recent crisis and their desire to promote security and reassert control. First, they reorganized Lincoln County's slave patrols and ordered them to extend their jurisdiction into "any part of Capt. Alexander's District," presumably because they felt this area needed special policing. Even if the local panic proved false, the White leadership was determined to make patrols more vigilant in their operations as a precaution. So White fears persisted.

The county also ordered Colonel John Hoke and Lincolnton attorney Carlos Leonard "to have such repairs done to the whipping post as they may deem necessary or have them made new" and also "to make such repairs to the Courthouse as they deem necessary." These repairs reflected the White population's resolve to bolster control and power. The whipping post was a powerful symbol of the political establishment and an important public method of punishment. The courthouse was the central seat of governmental authority and, during the preceding panic, a principal place of refuge for many of Lincolnton's most prominent women.

When Frank Rankin wrote his account of the Negro

War, he made no mention of Nat Turner's Rebellion and was likely unaware of the connection between the two events. However, the Southampton insurrection was the direct cause of the panic in Lincoln County. The local White population was scared out of its wits and falsely concluded the murderous uprising had spread to its doorstep. Even after the panic subsided, White masters remained afraid, now more aware than ever that their enslaved people could rise up and kill them, just as in Southampton County. However, unlike members of the White population, who used the local militia to protect themselves, enslaved persons were unarmed and vulnerable. White masters and their armed militia enjoyed the privilege of almost killing their innocent enslaved workers during the false insurrection scare. During the panic, both enslaved persons and White women and children found themselves confined. The former as temporary prisoners. The latter as refugees. Neither were free or secure. At every level, a society that embraced enslaved labor was one in which both the master class and enslaved people lived in steady, regular fear.

Frank Rankin's historical account of Lincoln County's "Negro War" is both humorous and terrifying. With pitchforks and clubs for weapons, and one militiaman wearing spurs on his bare feet, some militia members appear completely ridiculous. From that perspective, the account fits well into the Southern tradition of frontier humor. Told from the frame of reference of the frightened, misguided White militia to which his father belonged, Rankin's narrative is lively and interesting. However, throughout the piece, his narrator's voice and his father's first-person account are overtly supremacist and racially callous.

One can only imagine how differently the enslaved

victims—falsely accused, locked up without cause, and nearly killed—interpreted the same events. For enslaved Blacks, the false panic underscored a frightening realization. Anxious, uneasy White people held the power of life and death over their lives. And White security mattered more to owners of enslaved people than Black lives. These Lincoln County enslaved persons barely escaped, almost wrongly executed because of mistaken White fears. Read from the viewpoint of the falsely suspected enslaved people, the account is a chilling reminder of the violence and injustice of slavery.

For more about the High Shoals Iron Works and the early iron industry, see Lester J. Cappon, "Iron Making: A Forgotten Industry for North Carolina," *North Carolina Historical Review* 9 (October 1932): 331–48. Also see Robert N. Elliott, "The Nat Turner Insurrection as Reported in the North Carolina Press," *North Carolina Historical Review* 38 (January 1961): 1–18, and Charles Edward Morris, "Panic and Reprisal: Reaction in North Carolina to the Nat Turner Insurrection, 1831," *North Carolina Historical Review* 62 (January 1985): 29–52.

7

Wondering about the Wart Doctor

There are several reasons I believe my father Dr. Richard Rankin, a highly respected family doctor, was willing to refer his patients to Buck Starrett, a folk healer, to cure their warts. Because Dad grew up on a nearby farm and was thoroughly immersed in local culture, he was likely exposed to folk customs. He was also an imminently practical person who cared more about results than methods. Practicing in the small textile town of Mt. Holly, Dad routinely referred his patients to physician specialists in nearby Charlotte. Seeking help from others better equipped to treat his patients was his well-established pattern. And since having warts was not a serious or life-threatening condition, the risks were low. But my father was also skeptical and made decisions only after careful observation. He was a good doctor. So one of the most remarkable things about this story is that my father chose to send his patients to Cleveland Parks "Buck" Starrett, a local country store owner and occasional folk healer. And it worked. Their warts went away.

Dad learned about Mr. Starrett from his two longtime associates and close family friends, Ellen Featherstone, laboratory technician, and Gladys Reece, receptionist and record keeper. By the mid-1970s, Dr. Rankin, Miss Featherstone, and Mrs. Reece had worked together for more than a decade and formed a loyal, effective team.

Featherstone and Reece were next-door neighbors from nearby Cramerton, another small textile town. Mr. Starrett lived a few miles away in a house attached to his country store. They heard about and believed in his ability to cure warts, knew he was a good man, and told my father about him. By the early 1970s, Dad began giving patients who came for wart removal a choice: either they could pay him to excise or use acid to burn off their warts, leaving a scar, or they could go to Mr. Starrett for no charge, and their warts would disappear without a trace.

I remember my skepticism when my father first told us he was sending patients to Mr. Starrett. The whole thing sounded sort of crazy. But soon enough, the situation became very real and personal. When I was about seventeen years old, I developed a sizable, unsightly wart around the entire cuticle on one of my fingers, either index or middle of the right hand. The wart was embarrassingly ugly. Because it was so large and in such a prominent place, I constantly noticed and felt it. So I spoke to Dad about taking it off. By this time, he had already sent many patients to Buck Starrett, who successfully cured their warts. Without hesitation, my father told me to go see Mr. Starrett. It was useless to argue. Dad would never do anything that was not best for me.

Because my visit to Mr. Starrett happened so long ago, my memories of certain details are indistinct, but the main points remain clear. My sister Kitty and I knew Mr. Starrett's store well because we drove past it twice a day on our way to and from Gaston Day School. I cannot be certain whether we already stopped occasionally at Starrett's store for gasoline and snacks or whether we began going after my visit to have my wart removed. However, I do distinctly recall my strong skepticism when—as we referred to it—I went to "have my wart talked off." A lifelong Presbyterian, as a boy I was taught about Jesus' miracles and the role that faith played in his healings. Let me state now unequivocally: even then, I accepted a scientific worldview and had no sure faith that Mr. Starrett was able to take off my warts. I was full of doubts and only went because my father told me to go. In hindsight, perhaps my father's faith was enough. Or perhaps Mr. Starrett did not require faith from the recipient for his healing gift to work.

It's been almost fifty years since I made the trip to Starrett's Grocery alone. I don't remember every detail of that trip, which lasted a few minutes at most, but I do remember entering the store somewhat sheepishly, unsure what to expect. Mr. Starrett greeted me kindly, approached me from the other side of the store's main glass counter, full of assorted candies, and asked how he could help. Mrs. Starrett was there too, seated toward the back of the large, single-room store. I told him my father Dr. Rankin had sent me to have my wart taken off, and showed him my finger. He received my request nonchalantly and told me to pick out a gift. I was puzzled and asked, "What gift do I need to pick out?" He replied, "You can pick out anything you want." In hindsight, I am curious about what Mr. Starrett would have done had I requested an expensive item, and I suspect he would have given it to me. Instead, I asked, "Will a Mary Jane work?" "Yes," he said, reaching into the candy counter and handing me the small piece of molasses taffy in the red-and-yellow wrapper. I have always wondered why Mr. Starrett made picking a gift a requirement in the wart removal and wish I had asked. I speculate that giving a gift somehow actualized and acknowledged his own healing gift. But this is pure conjecture. Too young, embarrassed, and self-absorbed at the time, I can think now of many other questions I wish I had posed. How did he discover his healing gift? Did someone else teach him? How old was he when he started curing warts? Did he consider his gift to be a Christian one? How exactly did he do it?

After giving me the candy, Mr. Starrett said nothing else. Surprised that the wart-healing procedure was so simple and straightforward, I asked Mr. Starrett, "Don't you have to touch it?" Again, matter-of-factly, he responded, "I can if you want me to." I said, "Yes, I do," somehow thinking that there had to be a more elaborate technique to this exchange. So I stuck out my finger on the counter, and Mr. Starrett brushed it quickly and almost dismissively. I asked, "That's all?" He smiled and said, "Yes." I asked further, "And my wart will go away?" He smiled, nodded, and said, "Yes." With his last affirmation, our interaction ended. I thanked him, then turned and walked out of the store. The whole visit lasted less than two minutes and seemed completely practical, commonplace, and underwhelming. I neither felt nor sensed anything different or unusual during the entire encounter. Mr. Starrett was as down-to-earth and unassuming as if I had asked him to pump gas into my car, which he did occasionally. For a long time, I kept the Mary Jane candy in my valuables box in the bedroom.

The disappearance of my wart is the most mysterious thing about the whole episode. I bet I looked down at my finger one hundred times a day for the first week. There sat my ugly wart unchanged. I seriously doubted whatever Mr. Starrett did was going to be effective. But I did look. So, at some level, I wondered if it might work. And then—and this still amazes me—I stopped looking at my wart for perhaps a week. There is no good explanation for why I did so, and I must confess that this period of unconscious inattention has always seemed strange and wonderful. A week or so later, when I finally did remember to glance at my hand, the wart was gone. No trace. No scar. My finger was completely healed. I will always wonder what in the world happened and how Mr. Starrett did it. At a later date, my sister Kitty went to Mr. Starrett to heal her wart with a similarly successful result.

Throughout the succeeding years of my life, I occasionally told others about my experience with Mr. Starrett, and my audience has always been fascinated by two elements: first, that my father, a physician, referred his patients to a faith healer and, second, that my wart really went away.

In 2001, when I moved back to Gastonia to become Gaston Day Head of School more than twenty-five years after Mr. Starrett cured my wart, I found myself driving past his former store fairly often, which naturally caused me to wonder whatever happened to him. The structure now belonged to the United Baptist Church and was a youth fellowship building. The church sign out front still designated the place as "the Store" in reference to its previous history. Every time I passed the converted church annex, I thought about our shared past. Somehow it seemed appropriate that the old store was now part of a Baptist church, and I wondered if Mr. Starrett's healing gift was an expression of some deeper piety or holiness. I passed the building occasionally for twenty years without learning more.

Sometime in the last year (2021), I told my longtime executive assistant and friend, Rebekah Bing, about Mr. Starrett. Well, true to my previous experiences of sharing my wart story with others, she was entertained and fascinated and began encouraging me to find out what happened to him. So, after all these years, I found myself wondering if it was possible. I correctly assumed he was no longer living since I knew him fifty years earlier when he was already an older man. Buck Starrett died thirty-five years ago in 1987.

Several weeks before Christmas, I called the United Baptist Church, spoke to the church secretary, and asked if she was aware of anyone still alive who knew Mr. Starrett or was related to him (at this time I didn't even know his first or middle name). The church secretary was old enough to have known Mr. Starrett, and therefore the details of my request made sense. Also, when you tell somebody—even a stranger—that Mr. Starrett cured your warts, you immediately have their attention. Glad to help, the secretary told me that Mr. Starrett's daughter, Joan Starrett Motes, was still living near the store right down Titman Road. She had no further contact information. I was surprised and thrilled to get such a close, solid lead. A Google search quickly gave me Mrs. Motes's post office box and street address.

Over the following weeks, I failed to reach Joan Motes. Letters introducing myself and my interest in her father's story went unanswered. As a last-ditch effort, I decided to drive to her physical address to see if she still lived there. When I arrived and walked up to the place, the house was not only unoccupied but also under renovation. Obviously, she no longer lived there, and new owners were moving in soon. I was too late. Fortunately, there was a car next door at the neighbor's house, and I pulled in to continue my search. A man in his early forties answered the door, told me that Mrs. Motes moved to Hickory to be with her son David, forty miles away, and gave me her son's phone number. I drove barely 300 yards down the road before coming to a stop in the next parking lot to make the call. When David Motes answered, I explained my reason for contacting him. He chuckled, acknowledging that, yes, his grandfather had indeed cured people's warts at the store, and further observed, "I think you might be a little late in the game." I responded, "Better late than never." Then I asked him some of the questions I wish I had asked his grandfather. "Do you know when your grandfather first discovered he could cure warts? Do you know who taught him?" "No," he replied to both. "Did your grandfather consider taking off warts to be a Christian gift?" "I don't know." "Was Mr. Starrett a Christian?" "Of course." After speaking for just a few minutes, David Motes agreed to organize a meeting and introduce me to other family members who might be able to tell me more about Buck Starrett and his ability to cure warts.

On February 12, 2022, David Motes, his wife Janice Motes, and four other family members met me at Gaston Day to share memories of Buck Starrett. Remarkably, Jo Anne Bryant, who grew up next door to the Starretts and whose brother married Joan Starrett, *did not even know that Buck Starrett could heal warts.* Her total lack of knowledge indicates how little fanfare was associated with Starrett's healing gift. David and Janice Motes were well aware of Starrett's ability but knew almost nothing else about it. Curing the warts of people who came in the store was just something Buck Starrett always did. Janice Motes added that Starrett could also cure hiccups and dowse for water, two other folk customs that have no scientific explanation.

Talking to David and Janice Motes and Jo Anne Bryant

quickly revealed that Buck Starrett was not the only person they knew with healing and dowsing gifts. Mr. Armstrong (first name forgotten), another neighbor who lived on a farm right below the Starretts' store, cured Jo Anne Bryant's "seed wart" when she was a young adult. Nobody knows whether Mr. Armstrong taught Buck Starrett to cure warts. Janice Motes is herself a water dowser, but she did not learn it from Starrett. Rural neighborhoods in the North Carolina Piedmont often included people who had folk gifts of healing and divination. Buck Starrett was just one of them.

Everyone attending the interview expressed great love for Buck and his wife Lessie Norris Starrett and recalled how much they loved each other and their family. In particular, recollections about Buck Starrett revolved around his kindness, outgoing personality, and keen sense of humor. Both the Starrett and the Motes families belonged to the McAdenville Wesleyan Church, and church was central to their lives. But Buck Starrett was no puritan. He sold white liquor in the store and was an inveterate practical joker. He may really have been that rare individual who was mostly at peace with the world and his God and who enjoyed life fully. For his family, Buck Starrett's gifts of healing and divination were less significant aspects of his remarkably good life.

As our interview concluded, David Motes advised me to contact at least one more person: his 104-year-old great-uncle, Oscar Norris, who as a blind, middle-aged man after his wife's death had lived for nearly twenty years with the Starretts. Without sight for much of his adult life, Norris was still in sound mind and otherwise unusually good health for someone his age. When I phoned him at a nearby Gastonia assisted living center several days later to arrange our interview and introduced myself, he started the conversation by recalling, "Dr. Rankin sent his children to Buck to have their warts removed." "Yes," I replied, "and I am one of those children." Having a 104-year-old witness describe what happened to me almost 50 years earlier seemed almost incredible. Maybe Faulkner was right when he said, "The past is not dead. It's not even the past."

My meeting with Mr. Norris the next Saturday was much like my previous one with the family. He described Buck Starrett as "a good old boy" and fondly recalled his regular kindness. Well aware of Starrett's ability to cure warts, Norris told me that he kept strictly secret all information involving his gift. However, he did recall that Starrett chose "Wart Doctor" as his nickname or "handle" when he was on air as a Citizens Band Radio operator. So Mr. Starrett obviously took some measure of pride in his unusual talent.

Oscar Norris produced one big surprise in our interview when he mentioned that he went to Cramerton Elementary School with Gladys Reece, my father's longtime receptionist/secretary, and asked if she was still alive. He was so pleased to learn she was. The two of them are certainly the last surviving members of their class—she is only a few months short of 104 years old.

Reconnecting with Gladys Reece, whom I had not seen during the pandemic, was a happy reunion. At 103, she is still cheerful and keenly interested in others and what's happening in the world. Earlier in her professional life when she learned that Mr. Starrett could remove warts, she told my father. At first, Dad kept quiet about his referrals out of concern for what other doctors might think. But he lost any sense of shame or embarrassment as Mr. Starrett cured more and more of his patients. Mrs. Reece described Buck Starrett as a "jolly," kind person. Like everyone else interviewed, she knew almost nothing about the particulars of his ability to cure warts.

Those who knew Buck Starrett best remember his loving spirit, not his ability to heal warts. For his family and friends, love was his greatest legacy. But for me, as someone whose wart he cured, I will always wonder about the nature of his healing power. He shared his gift freely with others but refused to disclose its source or process. Wonder is born out of uncertainty and a deep longing to know the truth. It occupies a space somewhere between belief, doubt, and hope. We come to wonder whenever our limited human understanding meets an impenetrable mystery. After all these years and my own inconclusive investigation into the matter, my encounter with Mr. Starrett remains unforgettable, inexplicable, and wonderful.

8

The Folk Historian of Rankintown

Our relationship started fifteen years ago and involved a mutual enthusiasm for the hyper-local history of Rankintown, a once vibrant but now disintegrated rural community named for my family. Ash Spratt grew up during the late 1940s and 1950s, before family farming completely disappeared, and lived in Rankintown until his recent death. He had an almost visceral connection to the local landscape. He also retained an older attitude that land ownership was still the principal measure of an individual's stature and worth. Especially during the last forty years of his life, almost everyone else who remembered historic Rankintown as an important local agricultural community either moved away or died off.

Our families always knew each other. Spratt respected my father as a doctor, and Dad once sewed up a gash in his ankle when he was a young boy. Spratt's stepfather, Zeb Spratt Jr., ran a successful lawn care business and occasionally did work for my parents. Although Spratt and I bumped into each other a few times growing up, we only became well acquainted after 2007 when my wife, children and I moved back to our old family property, no longer a working farm. Spratt reintroduced himself and asked if he could fish in our pond, and thus began our friendship.

Ash Spratt and I may well have been the last two people who cared passionately about Rankintown's past. He was a folk historian, and I am a trained one. With a high school diploma from nearby Belmont's segregated Reid High School, the reality was that Spratt knew vastly more about Rankintown's history than I ever will. He carried all this information about the place and its land owners, especially during the last 100 years, mostly in his head. Related to many former residents, both Black and White, in his youth he roamed almost every acre of the area. He had lived in and through the place's history. In contrast, I grew up six miles away in Mt. Holly, with the Rankin farm as a second home, and studied family genealogy and local history more in the abstract. He was a witness, and I was much more of a student.

Spratt gained his knowledge of family and local history from several sources. First were his lived experiences as a boy growing up in Rankintown before its agricultural character was lost. Second was his dependence on the Black community's oral tradition. In this regard, Spratt participated in a folk history tradition that stretched all the way back to the ancient West African griots. He also valued and collected documentary evidence related to his family where he could find it. This included not only land deeds and surveys but also copies of census records and family photographs.

Spratt was drawn to anyone interested in Rankintown history. Decades before he and I became acquainted, he befriended Eleanor Spratt Hacker (1912–1999), my distant Rankin cousin and student of family history. Mrs. Hacker lived with her two unmarried sisters in a fine antebellum house located at the southern end of historic Rankintown.

She and her sisters were directly descended from Rankintown's largest pre-Civil War owner of land and enslaved people, and they retained extensive family land. Their Rankin family papers are housed in the University of North Carolina at Chapel Hill's Southern Historical Collection and chronicle that branch of the family, especially dealing with the period from 1865 to 1995.

As a mixed-race person, Ash Spratt was unflinching in describing the ways in which Whites historically took advantage of Rankintown's Blacks and mixed-race people. He retained property surveys for tracts that Zeb Spratt Sr. once owned. Without ever producing any hard evidence, Ash Spratt believed his family had been defrauded out of Zeb Spratt Sr.'s landholdings. In Ash Spratt's mind, these "stolen" parcels were the most concrete examples of a larger pattern of land theft from his family. Spratt dreamed of legal maneuvers to recover specific Rankintown properties to which he believed his family was entitled.

Spratt believed he was the son of Robert Shipp, a mixed-race man related to the Rankins. Shipp grew up nearby off NC Hwy 27 on a tract of land long owned by his family. Spratt was six years old before he had any suspicion that Shipp was his father. By that time, Robert Shipp had died in an accidental drowning while living in New York state. Eventually in later years, Spratt's mother confirmed that Shipp was indeed his biological father. Zeb Spratt Jr. raised his stepson Ash Spratt as his own. Even after Ash Spratt became aware that Zeb Spratt Jr. was not his blood father, he related to him like one, called him "Daddy," and took his last name. As a result of having two fathers—one biological and one step, and both from families long settled around Stanley Creek—Ash Spratt felt kinship with many local families including the Shipps, the Spratts, and the Rankins. When recalling events farther back than a century ago, he tended to exaggerate the land holdings and influence of the White Rankin and Spratt families related to him.

According to copies of 1880 census records, Zeb Spratt Sr. and his Black wife were a biracial couple who had ten children, including several who passed for and married White people. Although Ash Spratt grew up in a segregated society that legally divided people into either White or Black, his own family consisted of a spectrum of White and mixed-race individuals. Their skin colors were white, dark brown, and every shade in between. Ash Spratt's own skin was the color of coffee ice cream. With so many biracial and White relatives, a clear-cut concept of race made no sense at all to him. While he had never been taught the scientific theory of race as a social construct with no biological meaning, as a practical matter he reached the same conclusion based on his own family's racial diversity. So while he lived primarily within the local Black community, he related easily to everyone including White Spratt and Rankin relatives. For him, the importance of family—even extended family—surpassed socially determined racial categories. And, ultimately, he evaluated people on their individual merits and character. Finally, despite our differences in background and racial attributions, Ash Spratt and I had so much in common that we couldn't help but like each other. He called me "cousin" or "cuz."

For the last fifteen years of his life, Ash Spratt and I interacted frequently, often simply greeting each other briefly when I drove past him and his buddies fishing on our pond. Occasionally, however, he would drive up to my house for a visit or bump into me out on my property, and then begin much longer discussions of Rankintown history. I also called him whenever any local history question arose, and he almost always knew the answer. For instance, learning that in the 1980s there was once an illegal chicken fighting pit near the intersection of the Lowland Dairy Road and Old NC Hwy 27, I asked him for more information. Not only did he know about it, but he was also aware of another popular fighting spot in the woods on the old Wyatt place just down the Lowland Dairy Road. The scope of his historical knowledge of Rankintown was vast.

After years of asking for a recorded interview to document his wealth of local lore, I finally convinced Spratt to come one recent Saturday morning. I now wonder if his willingness was prompted out of a premonition of his own death. The afternoon preceding our interview, he arrived unscheduled before I got home from work and, standing in our driveway, gave my uninitiated wife a fascinating forty-five-minute, stream-of-consciousness oral history. Because my wife lacked any immediate context from growing up in nearby Charlotte and away from Rankintown, she found Spratt's account hard to follow but listened patiently out of courtesy, respect, and an appreciation of his impressive fund of hyper-local lore. The next morning, Spratt returned, and he and I sat on the front porch for a recorded interview that lasted forty-six minutes and five seconds. He brought numerous family deeds and pictures with him. We laughed a lot as we enjoyed the pleasure of each other's company and our shared Rankintown past.

Following the interview, we drove my pickup truck around our home territory for about another forty-five minutes, and he pointed out places and things he wanted me to know. When we passed the old James Campbell Rankin homeplace, I asked Spratt if he knew about the Rankin Oak, one of the region's largest red oaks before it died sometime after the 1960s. *Of course he did. He had seen it many times.* Near the bottom end of our driving loop, he pointed out the location of the long-gone Rankintown Colored School near the South Stanley Creek bridge and asked if I had heard of it. Yes, but only as an abstract place name on a historic map. Spratt had actually been inside the old, abandoned building and knew people who attended school there.

At two places on our route, one near the former site of the Rankintown Colored School and another a half-mile farther up Old Hwy 27 toward Stanley, Spratt showed me where old Rankin family cemeteries had been located and noted that one contained a Union soldier's remains. As odd and out of place as a Yankee grave seemed in our family burial ground, it made sense because one phase of Stoneman's Union Raid at the end of the Civil War occurred around Rankintown, with a few casualties on both sides. Federal troops probably confiscated the burial plot for their dead comrade. About a mile farther up the same road, Spratt took me down Flat Top Lane to one of our oldest family home sites. The place was previously unknown to me and, perhaps, the original residence of John Davidson Rankin, Eleanor Hacker's wealthy ancestor and my distant relative. Throughout the whole informal historical tour, Spratt and I were completely at ease talking about our cherished, conflicted history—as always, me mostly learning from Ash Spratt.

Short of breath during much of the day we spent together, Spratt had not felt well for about a month and had an appointment to see the doctor in two days. A friend called four days after our meeting to tell me he died the following

Monday, two days after our visit. The viewing of his body was held at a Black funeral home in Gastonia exactly a week after our interview. Dressed in a handsome black suit, Spratt appeared asleep in the coffin. There was a large printed banner above the casket with a graphic image of Spratt playing the electric guitar, which he loved to do, and below it a generic pond scene. The banner reminded me of the many happy hours Spratt spent fishing on our pond. Because my grandson was being baptized out of town the next day, I missed the funeral.

Ash Spratt was a remarkably honest, decent, intelligent, likable, and interesting person. His enthusiasm for our neighborhood's hyper-local history reflected a deep curiosity about and affection for his home. He was Rankintown's most devoted native son. So much of its past vanishes with him. There is a gaping hole in the place, and I feel less confident to fully understand its history without him.

Rest in peace, Ash Spratt. No one knew more about Rankintown's complicated, problematic history than you. You honored me with your friendship. Our fellowship gives me hope that someday we can all live in amity and respect, overcoming past inequities to celebrate our common heritage, humanity, and kinship.

9

A Remembered Bird Hunting Landscape

In the last two decades of the nineteenth century and the first decades of the twentieth, the rural farming community of Rankintown in northeastern Gaston County was part of Piedmont North Carolina's outstanding regional bobwhite quail hunting landscape. From the 1880s to the 1920s, small farms like Willowside produced ideal quail habitat with their patchwork of grain and pea fields as feed and the bordering undergrowth and mixed woods as protective cover against predators. Late nineteenth-century technological improvements in shotgun manufacturing produced relatively inexpensive, reliable, and accurate hunting firearms. An extensive railroad network made the region accessible to hunting tourists. Until the 1920s, all these factors combined to make local bird hunting in the Piedmont popular and even attractive to northern sportsmen. Almost all local bird hunters either belonged or were connected to farming families like the Rankins with private lands available to hunt.

Willowside was located less than five miles away from both Mt. Holly and Stanley Creek and less than a mile north of the midpoint between the two towns on the Central Carolina Railroad. In 1886, a local newspaper noted that bird hunting in Stanley Creek was "one of the principal sources of amusement and diversion to our amateur sportsmen." Twelve years later in 1898, Seaboard Air Line Railroad's *The Sportsman's Guide* advertised "excellent" quail shooting on the Central Carolina near both Mt. Holly and Stanley Creek. The two towns offered local hunting guides, bird dogs, horses, and reasonably priced accommodations at hotels and boarding houses.

My grandfather Frank Bisaner Rankin, born in 1878, was likely the first family member to take up quail hunting at Willowside. As teenagers in the 1930s, my father Richard Rankin and his brother Frank Battley Rankin grew up bird hunting alongside neighborhood boys. More than once, Dad told me the story about one of these hunting buddies, who had an intellectual disability but was a shooting savant who could regularly hit a bobwhite in flight with a .22 rifle, not the standard shotgun. Anyone who has ever struggled to hit a quail on the wing with a full load of bird shot will understand why this true story about my father's sharpshooting friend is amazing.

Already by the time of my father and uncle's youths, top bobwhite quail hunting was gradually shifting south, away from the North Carolina Piedmont to more productive game lands in South Carolina and Georgia. By the end of World War II, the heyday of Piedmont quail hunting was over. The conversion of crop fields to fescue pastures, with thick grass that trapped quail chicks, may have been partly responsible for habitat changes that reduced Piedmont quail populations. After 1950, the gradual disappearance of family farms increased the slow, steady decline in wild birds.

Even with the North Carolina Piedmont's declining popularity as a quail hunting destination after the 1920s, local men still bird hunted around Mt. Holly and Stanley (in the 1920s the town dropped the "Creek" from its name and became just "Stanley"). Indeed, the local bird hunting culture was vibrant enough to produce at least two regionally respected dog trainers: Oliver Shook of Stanley and Paschal DeWayne "Pat" Moore of Mt. Holly. At various times, both men handled field trial dogs for Olin Eugene "O. E. or Bo" Massey, Mt. Holly hardware merchant, prominent field trial man, and my father's future hunting partner. Eventually, in 1964, my father and Bo Massey started the Quail Roost Hunt Club, a private quail hunting club 150 miles away in Clarendon County, South Carolina, where bird hunting was better. Through Bo Massey, my father knew Pat Moore well and almost certainly Oliver Shook.

By 1936, Oliver Shook was breeding and selling registered English pointers. Over his career, he developed a well-known line of black-and-white or "rip-rap" pointers, one of which he sold for top dollar to William Wrigley of the Chicago chewing gum fortune. I never met Oliver Shook, although he was a close friend and dog-training associate of Joe McCall, our dog trainer and caretaker at the Quail Roost Hunt Club in South Carolina.

Pat Moore lived right next door to Bo Massey on North Main Street in Mt. Holly and maintained his kennel there. Every hunting season for more than twenty-five years, Pat and his wife Wilma Thompson Moore went to Clarendon County, South Carolina, where he trained dogs and guided bird hunts at a private preserve and she cooked for guest hunters. At the end of each hunting season, the Moores returned to their primary residence in Mt. Holly. After a showcase trial hunt at the Clarendon County hunting preserve where the Moores worked, in the early 1980s I bought a lemon-and-white male English pointer from Pat Moore to be used at the Quail Roost Hunt Club.

I only bird hunted at our farm property around Willowside a few times, and never after the early 1970s when I started going to the Quail Roost Hunt Club. The first bird hunt I remember was with my father and our farm manager John Haggins when I was too young to carry a gun. We hunted a series of small broomsedge fields growing on the back side of our property and found a single large covey. A few years later, Dad, Mr. Haggins, and I went bird hunting again, this time in the fields and pastures around Willowside, and found several coveys. I distinctly remember my father shooting a covey rise near a long multiflora rose hedge on the border of our largest pasture. My last farm bird hunt as a teenager was with my Uncle Bill Jarman in the early 1970s. He brought his bird dogs, and we killed several quail out of a covey in a small pasture just below the farm pond. By that time, Bill Jarman had succeeded O. E. Massey as my father's partner at our South Carolina hunting club, where we hunted often together.

After 1970, as a young teenager focused exclusively on bird hunting at the Quail Roost Hunt Club in South Carolina with my father and others, I completely lost touch with quail hunting on the Rankin farm where our family's bird hunting tradition originated and whose lands my father still owned and used as a beef cattle operation. The local bobwhite population continued to decline around Willowside, but huntable numbers remained until the early 1980s, and each spring male birds could be heard calling to female mates. But with better hunting grounds in Clarendon County and our bird dogs stationed there during hunting season, there was no time or reason to hunt on our family property in Gaston County.

By the mid-1980s, landscape-scale changes in quail

habitat across the Southeastern United States, many of them related to the loss of family farming, caused a precipitous drop in wild bird populations. Bobwhite quail numbers plummeted in the two Carolinas and throughout most of the Southeast. My father, my uncle Bill Jarman, his son Dr. Bill Jarman Jr., and I experienced this painful decline up close in Clarendon County. In 1985, with the wild birds nearly gone, we sold the Quail Roost Hunt Club to deer hunters from Florida. Preoccupied with our own deteriorating situation in South Carolina during these final years, for us the end of the wild bird era around Stanley and Mt. Holly happened almost completely out of sight and mind. The bobwhites were vanishing there too, even if we didn't see it ourselves.

I saw the last bobwhites on our northeastern Gaston County family property in the 1990s. In April 1993, while hiking with my four-year-old son, we jumped a wild covey and saw where the singles landed in a bunch. At my suggestion, we decided to go flush them. My son, who was armed with a wooden toy sword and a rubber knife, gave me his sword and instructed me to swing it when the birds got up, and he would do the same with his knife. That's exactly what we did. The explosive sound of the bobwhites taking flight excited and startled my young son so much that he started screaming wildly while brandishing his rubber knife. Since these bobwhites were located near the now overgrown pasture below the pond where Uncle Bill Jarman and I hunted in the early 1970s, they may well have been descended from the same covey.

In January 1994 while I was alone hiking on the family property, our two black labs jumped another small covey. Five years later in January 1999, driving up the road to the cabin on our property, I flushed four quail, probably getting grist, and watched a cock and hen for several minutes as they lit not far away. Once again, these birds were near the overgrown pasture below the pond. This was the last time I saw a bobwhite quail on Rankin property.

Accepting the loss of wild birds has been difficult, and every time I drive through our property, I keep hoping to see one. Not hearing bobwhite mating calls each spring seems sadly unnatural. But the whole agricultural world that supported quail is no more. Former crop fields are either planted in loblolly pines or have reverted to wildwoods. The overgrown landscape no longer resembles the neat farmlands once dotted with grain fields and pastures. No wonder the quail have vanished.

Bobwhites are not completely extinct in Gaston County. Where the landscape is right, a few wild birds persist. Less than five miles from our family property, the Mountain Island Educational State Forest has open pinelands with an understory that is periodically cleared with prescribed burning. This creates a habitat that supports several coveys of bobwhite quail. Today, places conducive to wild birds are uncommon in a largely post-agricultural Piedmont North Carolina. Quail hunting as a sport is only practiced on shooting preserves where pen-raised birds are either released in large numbers before the season starts or put out by preserve staff immediately before the day's hunt begins. Only older people remember wild birds, and nobody hunts them anymore.

In 2018, then in my early sixties, I published a memoir, *While There Were Still Wild Birds: A Personal History of Southern Quail Hunting*, recounting my family's involvement in the last two decades of wild bird hunting in South Carolina at the Quail Roost Hunt Club. One surprising result has been the number of old bird hunters who have contacted me either to discuss their own hunting experiences or buy copies of my book. I never imagined one of them would be from my home territory of northeastern Gaston County during the 1970s: the precise period of time when South Carolina hunting was removing me from the local quail hunting scene. But that is exactly what happened when Stanford E. "Stan" Baker—whom I did not know previously—called me at work one day last year (2021) to ask where he could buy my book. When I told him that I had some signed copies at school, Baker drove right over from his home nearby to make the purchase.

My meeting with Stan Baker that day lasted much longer than expected as he shared bird hunting memories from the 1970s near our family farm and other places close by, and we began to make connections between our families and ourselves. A lengthier interview with him followed later. Baker, then sixty-eight years old, grew up in our hometown of Mt. Holly. His stories about the final decade of quail hunting in eastern Gaston County, North Carolina, brought me as close as possible to the end of wild bird hunting around our own family property.

Growing up in the same small town and with so many things in common, it really is remarkable that Stan Baker and I never previously met. Three years older than me, he had lived with his family on North Hawthorne Street in Mt. Holly and attended the local public schools. Baker's father owned a successful public accounting firm, and my father was a town doctor. So our parents were well acquainted. One of Baker's cousins was my close childhood friend. But our families lived several miles apart and belonged to different churches, I started attending a private school twelve miles away in the fifth grade, and somehow we remained unacquainted. Maybe the age gap was just enough to keep us separated in community activities like Little League, Pee Wee football, and Cub Scouts. If we had been friends as teenagers, we might well have bird hunted together at the Rankin farm and other good spots Baker knew.

Also previously unfamiliar to me was another strong tie between the Bakers and the Rankins: our families were farming neighbors for several generations. The original 180-acre Baker farm adjoined the old James C. Rankin farm next to ours. Baker's grandparents lived on a 12-acre outparcel of the older, larger Baker farm property. Although Stan Baker grew up in town, he remained directly connected to the shrinking rural world around Mt. Holly and Stanley through his grandparents Raymond and Lucy Baker. He first learned to quail hunt at their place, less than two miles from our ancestral homestead. While he never bird hunted on our farm, once as a teenager Baker snuck into our largest pasture to shoot doves.

In the same way that Baker knew our family land, I had driven past his grandparents' place on the way to the Rankin farm and peered down the power line that traversed the property my whole life without ever knowing who owned it. Because I was similarly acquainted with the other places Baker described, I could practically imagine myself bird hunting alongside him. There was an amazing coincidence in where Baker's bird hunting took place, my own knowledge of the local landscape, and my great desire to learn more about the last decade of local quail hunting. His stories felt especially meant for me.

Stan Baker started small game hunting as a twelve- or thirteen-year-old. He first hunted squirrels with his father in an old hardwood stand on Bowater Corporation's pulpwood lands behind his grandparents' land. From ages twelve to fifteen, Baker kept two beagles and hunted rabbits at his grandparents' place and across Old Hwy 27 on neighboring lands. This small game hunting and caring for dogs prepared him for what happened next. One summer Saturday as a fifteen-year-old, as usual at his grandparents', Stan Baker found an abandoned male liver-and-white English pointer wandering the property without a collar. Although Baker knew about bird dogs, this was the first one he had ever seen. After petting and playing with his new friend for several minutes, Baker took the bird dog several hundred yards down a dirt road toward his grandfather's pea patch. About halfway there, the dog scented birds and went on point. Seeing a bird dog point for the first time in his life surprised and fascinated Baker, and he decided to keep the orphaned dog. Unfortunately, the following hunting season, he learned why his dog had been abandoned in the first place: it was gun-shy (the term for a hunting dog that is terrified and disoriented after hearing a gunshot). In the bigger scheme of things, this setback barely affected Baker's growing enthusiasm for quail hunting. He was hooked.

Two years later when he was seventeen years old, Baker bought his first bird dog, a registered female liver-and-white English pointer. Eldreth Lewis, a breeder and trainer who lived on the South Point Road outside nearby Belmont, sold it to him. Baker named his dog "Fidest," giving it his grandfather Baker's middle name, and he trained the six-month-old puppy himself. There was a huge, single covey of about thirty quail on the edge of his Mt. Holly neighborhood off Old Mine Road near the municipal pool, and this was where Baker took Fidest every afternoon. By the following hunting season, Fidest was fully "broke," which in bird dog parlance meant she was able to find quail, hold a point, and retrieve any bobwhites that were shot. Baker and Fidest were ready to start bird hunting.

Typically on a Saturday during bird season, usually in the afternoon, Baker put Fidest in the trunk of his 1963 Dodge and drove the three miles to his grandparents' land off Old NC Hwy 27. He shot the 16-gauge part of a German drilling gun (a custom-made firearm with a side-by-side double barrel shotgun over a .22 rifle) that his father brought back from World War II. There was only one covey on his grandparents' side of Old 27, and it could be found in any of several places. Usually alone and always on foot with Fidest, Baker followed a set course. He started around his grandfather's single cultivated field, often with harvested corn stalks still standing, and sometimes found the covey there. Moving down the power line, there was a broomsedge field above Stanley Creek that also frequently held the covey. Another choice spot was the power line at the edge of his grandfather's property, and here the birds were especially likely to be on the roost early in the morning. If flushed off the roost, these birds had to be shot on the covey rise before escaping into a thick, impenetrable briar patch further down the power line.

After hunting for the single covey on his grandparents' side of Old 27, Baker followed the power line as it climbed the hill and crossed the highway onto properties belonging to his cousin Yates Baker and Mr. Gus Broome. This section contained a second covey, and sometimes these birds foraged right out in the power line right of way. At other times, they stayed in two small broomsedge fields off the power line or in oak woods between these fields. Especially late in the afternoon, this second group of birds liked to sunbathe in the oak woods before flying to the roost. Baker quickly learned where to take Fidest to give the best chance of finding these quail.

With only two coveys total, the hunt at his grandparents' place was a far cry from a high-dollar South Georgia quail hunt that boasted thirty-plus coveys a day. But for seventeen-year-old Stan Baker, afield with Fidest, this was the real thing. From his house on Hawthorne Street, it took less than ten minutes to get there. The hunting was free, and his grandparents and the neighbors were always glad to see him. He and Fidest usually found one or two coveys, often with some extra singles shooting thrown in. Grandmother Lucy Baker always treated him by baking a delicious quail pot pie with the birds he killed. The Old 27 hunt was familiar, reliable, and beautiful, and it became Stan Baker's "go-to" bird hunt.

Over the next several years in the early 1970s, Baker added three more local half-day bird hunts to his regular rotation. With more places available, he hunted at least every other Saturday for the entire quail season, from early November until the end of February. The best of these new hunts began inside Mt. Holly's town limits in the Woodland Park neighborhood and then proceeded north of town through pinelands and broomsedge fields parallel to NC Highway 273 and the railroad spur that carried coal to two steam-station power plants. Two major power lines intersected on the back half of the hunt, creating additional hunting habitat. One of these power lines was the same one that crossed Baker's grandparents' property several miles away on the other side of Dutchmans Creek.

Baker started his Woodland Park-NC Hwy 273 hunt where Dogwood Drive dead ends at a cable barrier near the railroad spur on the neighborhood's northeastern edge. Because my best boyhood friend Parker Whitt lived in Woodland Park during these same years, he and I frequently explored the area around this cable barrier and occasionally hiked about a mile up the pinelands that Baker hunted further north. In the early 1970s, Whitt remembers often scattering bobwhite quail while riding his mini-bike around the neighborhood, and he heard quail calling in springtime from his house in the middle of Woodland Park. Although the wild bird population was declining, bobwhites still were present on the town's outskirts.

The Woodlark Park-NC Hwy 273 bird hunt held three coveys. Fidest often pointed birds several hundred yards north of the cable barrier in a patch of pines between the railroad spur and the river. Even more regularly, Baker and Fidest found a second covey about two miles up Hwy 273 in the open pines and scattered honeysuckle thickets around the Duke Power Training Center. This habitat was ideal, and the pinewood covey may have been the most reliable among all the ones that Baker hunted locally. Unfortunately, in 1979, the construction of the Freightliner Truck manufacturing plant destroyed these pinewoods and forced the bobwhite covey to leave.

There was one final covey often to be found on the NC 273 hunt. They ranged broadly in the broomsedge under the two power lines that intersect near the Cox family property. This was the northern terminus of the Woodland Park-Hwy 273 hunt. From here, Baker reversed his course down one of the power lines and hunted back to his car at the end of

Dogwood Drive, sometimes finding one of the coveys that he had missed on his way up the hunt.

In 1972 as a high school senior, Stan Baker bought his second English pointer from classmate Frank Carlton, another young bird hunter who lived just outside Stanley on the Lucia highway. Carlton owned a female liver-and-white pointer with a litter of puppies, including one black-and-white or "rip-rap" female. Black-and-white was a much less common color for English pointers than liver-and-white or lemon-and-white. Only once before had Baker ever seen another black-and-white pointer, bumping into the dog and its hunter-owner while afield north of Woodland Park. Even in such a single, brief encounter, Baker found this bird dog's color unusually attractive. In a similar way, he fancied the distinctive markings of the one rip-rap puppy in Carlton's litter. So he picked it out at the price of twenty dollars. Baker named his new puppy "Lucy" after his grandmother Baker, who was not the least bit pleased to have a bird dog named after her.

When Stan Baker told me about his black-and-white pointer during our interview, I asked if he knew about Oliver Shook, who also lived in Stanley and bred the well-known line of "rip-rap" pointers. But he did not. While there is no way to be sure, I suspect both the black-and-white pointer that Baker saw hunting off Hwy 273 and the puppy he bought from Frank Carlton came out of the same line of bird dogs. If so, Shook's rip-raps added their distinctive appearance and fine hunting instincts to succeeding generations of local bird dogs.

Just as with Fidest, Stan Baker trained his new puppy Lucy on the Old Mine Road covey. He now owned two bird dogs, Fidest and Lucy, but always chose to hunt them separately. One of Baker's most memorable bird hunts with Lucy happened at John L. and Frances Currence's property off Westland Farm Road between Mt. Holly and Stanley. The Currences were close family friends, and they allowed Baker to bird hunt their place whenever he liked. Because my Pee Wee football team practiced in the Currences' front field when I was a boy, I knew the property well.

On one particularly memorable hunt at the Currences' place, Baker started Lucy near a broomsedge field behind the pond at the front of the property. He was now shooting a 20-gauge Remington Model 1100 automatic shotgun bought at Mt. Holly Farm Supply. When Lucy pointed a covey, Baker shot one bird on the covey rise, and the rest of the single birds flew into an adjoining fescue field. As the bird dog moved into and worked the field, she pointed the first single, and Baker hit it on the rise. She did the same thing three more times, and Baker knocked down three more birds. Having already killed five out of the fifteen or so birds in the covey, Baker decided to stop and leave the remaining quail as seed birds for the future.

The last of Stan Baker's four local bird hunts was located along two power lines just on the other side of the Catawba River from Mt. Holly on Lake Drive in Mecklenburg County. Here in the early 1970s, his father bought the family a river cabin located close to the power lines, and Stan Baker discovered another good bird hunt. He hunted the power lines in two sections. The first was within walking distance of the river cabin and extended south for about a mile and a half to NC Highway 27. Two coveys worked this area. After hunting the first half of the river cabin hunt, Baker often drove a few miles away and parked off Belmeade Drive to continue hunting on one of the same power lines after it crossed NC 27 and ran south toward Interstate 85. One more quail covey foraged in this second stretch. Today, the US National Whitewater Center parking lot occupies part of this same power line right-of-way.

Stan Baker stopped bird hunting in 1979. The main reason was because he took up a new hobby, weightlifting, which consumed his free weekend time. But it was also true that the local quail population had decreased significantly, and birds were becoming scarcer and harder to find. Baker gave Lucy to a family in the nearby Coulwood community, and they turned her into a pet. Fidest lived another two years before dying in 1981. A decade later in 1991, Baker bought a German shorthaired pointer and resumed bird hunting. But the wild bird hunting era was over in Gaston County, and Baker's only option was shooting pen-raised quail at a commercial preserve to the west in Cleveland County. All across the North Carolina Piedmont, Baker's situation was being repeated as the disappearance of wild birds forced quail hunters to either discontinue their cherished field sport or go to shooting preserves with released quail.

The landscape that Stan Baker bird hunted has been irreparably altered in the intervening years. Not only are almost all the old farm fields overgrown or planted in loblolly pines, but many of his other hunting areas have been heavily developed. On the Woodland Park-NC Hwy 273 hunt, just above Dogwood Drive, now sits the large River Park residential housing development. Farther north, not only the Freightliner Truck manufacturing plant but also the National Gypsum Board manufacturing plant occupy a large chunk of the same hunt. Part of the Currence farm is now the large Westland Farm housing development. As mentioned previously, the US National Whitewater Center parking lot lies on the power line right-of-way where Baker hunted just off the Catawba River in Mecklenburg County. Even if wild birds somehow miraculously returned, these places can no longer be hunted. With explosive growth of the Charlotte metropolitan region, the pace of development in eastern Gaston County is only increasing. More of the old rural landscape will be lost over time.

Without Stan Baker's reminiscences, the final decade of wild bird hunting in eastern Gaston County would be indefinite. Instead, he remembers the specific details of favorite hunting grounds, prized bird dogs, and where some of the area's last bobwhites were located. His history as a solitary young sportsman completes and brings to a close the local 100-year-old bird hunting tradition. For me, his memories also suggest what was happening to the rest of the wild birds in Gaston County and, in particular, to the bobwhite quail on our farm so close to his grandparents' place.

In *While There Were Still Birds*, I describe the way quail hunting "transformed ordinary places...into hallowed grounds rich with experiences and full of meaning and memories." Stan Baker's hallowed hunting grounds were power line right-of-ways, broomsedge fields, and open pinewoods of eastern Gaston County. His memories are especially poignant because they recall an iconic game bird, a once prevalent field sport, and a remnant countryside, all of which have largely gone away. Without the quail, the local landscape is so much emptier and lonelier. Each spring, country people old enough to remember bobwhite mating calls mourn the silence and the lost rural world it signifies.

The first part of this essay, which discusses the last bobwhites on our family property, relies on *Rankintown Notes: A Journal of Minding and Mending Family Land, 1991–2003* (Gastonia, NC: Richard Rankin, 2010). The source for the second section is an interview with Stanford E. "Stan" Baker and the author on July 24, 2022. Also see Richard Rankin, *While There Were Still Wild Birds: A Personal History of Southern Quail Hunting* (Macon, GA: Mercer University Press, 2018).

10

An Attraction to Wildness

At eighty-seven years old, Henry Henkel Rhyne sat fit, ramrod-straight, and handsome in his downtown Mt. Holly office. Every inch the understated patrician, he reminded me of General Douglas MacArthur. Evidence of his outdoor life cluttered the space. Dog-eared sporting magazines lay scattered about. Dusty old turkey beards and small deer-antler mounts were displayed on the walls. So much smaller than today's enormous trophy racks, the vintage deer mounts came from a bygone era of sparse deer populations when hunters celebrated killing a buck of any size. A rich hunting history pervaded Rhyne's office. As a leader in the local land trust movement, I came to introduce one of the state's major commercial developers who was exploring the possibility of purchasing Mr. Rhyne's Sandy Ford farm as a private conservation preserve. Cool, confident, and self-possessed, Henry Rhyne sized up his prospects, and the deal never materialized.

Of course, everyone in our small North Carolina town knew about Henry Rhyne (1912–2003), even if they did not know him well: his family founded the town, and he himself was a textile scion, a successful businessman, and something of a colorful character. Our families had been friends for generations, and Dad was his family physician. My mother was a good friend of his second wife Bobbie Rhyne. In the late 1970s as a college student, I even attended a Christmas party at the Rhynes' home and saw Mr. Rhyne warmly hug my father's older sister Kitty Rankin Watson. After the party I asked my father whether Mr. Rhyne and Aunt Kitty were "old flames," and he confirmed that indeed they had been high school sweethearts. My Aunt Kitty Watson was a beautiful woman all her life. They would have been a stunning couple.

With all his local celebrity, our family connections, and even the brief encounter at the Christmas party, I barely knew Henry Rhyne. He was forty years older than me and only a strong family acquaintance through my parents. And I was completely ignorant of his sporting life. But seeing the office's hunting memorabilia, I immediately knew Henry Rhyne was one of the most experienced outdoorsmen I had ever met. Surely he had incredible stories to share, and I told myself that I was going to interview him and find out more. But I never did, and he died three years later. Not interviewing Henry Henkel Rhyne is a great regret. So many times while doing the research for this essay when encountering dead ends, I thought, "Why in the world did you not interview Henry Rhyne? He could have answered these questions so easily!"

My research has only convinced me more strongly that Henry Henkel Rhyne is the nearest thing Gaston County has to a modern-day Daniel Boone. He excelled as a woodsman, hunter, marksman, fisherman, trapper, mushroom gatherer, nature photographer, black powder enthusiast, and pioneer-skills craftsman and practitioner. Few people know about him or the extent of his accomplishments because he lived in a small town and spent so much time outdoors with a few close friends or alone. His story is fascinating because of his ability to balance—or perhaps juxtapose—an extraordinary life in nature with success in other, more practical areas. His remarkable sporting life also epitomized the rich opportunities for outdoor adventure and enjoyment available to someone of his background, ability, and means during a period of North Carolina's rapid growth—a process to which his family directly contributed and from which it benefited. But beyond these larger themes, Henry Henkel Rhyne's life is just plain interesting because he was such a talented, complicated, and colorful human being. Call him what you will—unique, one of a kind, *sui generis*—he was a North Carolina original.

Rhyne's grandfather Abel Peterson "A. P." Rhyne partnered with his father-in-law and brother to become one of North Carolina's first great textile manufacturing families. Rhyne Cotton Mills produced enormous wealth directed to other investments and good causes. Immediate family members endowed Lenoir-Rhyne College (which bears their name in Hickory, North Carolina), donated funds to build many Lutheran churches throughout the Piedmont, and reputedly owned the first automobile in North Carolina. Inherited wealth cascaded down several succeeding generations of the family. Unfortunately, Henry's father, Henry A. Rhyne, lost a significant portion of his inheritance in the Great Depression.

Rhyne's mother Alice Yount Henkel came from a prominent, wealthy Statesville, North Carolina, mercantile family. The Henkels were not only leading businessmen in Statesville (forty miles north of Charlotte) but also pioneers in developing Blowing Rock, North Carolina, as a mountain resort. They built the turnpike opening the village to tourism and owned and operated the then hugely popular and now historic Green Park Inn. Henry Henkel Rhyne was an only child but belonged to a large, cousin-filled family in both Mt. Holly and Blowing Rock. Through his extensive family network and all its friends and associates, Rhyne was exceptionally well connected to Piedmont North Carolina's business and social elite. These connections remained strong even after the Great Depression erased some of his family's wealth.

Henry Rhyne grew up in his parents' large, handsome home on North Main Street in Mt. Holly and lived there most of his life. The C. E. Hutchison mansion and estate—also derived from textile wealth—sat directly across the street. Rhyne attended Mt. Holly public schools, and his family worshiped at Good Shepherd Lutheran Church, about a block up Main Street toward the center of town. Only bits and pieces of his early development as a woodsman survive, and much must be inferred. He grew up less than one hundred yards from Dutchmans Creek, a Catawba River tributary where one of his grandfather's first cotton mills was situated (and still stands dilapidated), and less than two miles from the main channel of the Catawba, a major Piedmont river. Long stretches of woods, streams, and fields were just beyond his door. He did not like school, preferred to be outside, and became a hunter and a fisherman as a boy.

No one knows who taught Henry Rhyne to be a woodsman, and important parts of his early outdoor life remain obscure. His father and grandfather focused strictly on business. No one is sure if he learned to trap muskrats as a boy or later as an adult. Nobody is certain whether he read popular juvenile books by Ernest Seton Thompson or other outdoor juvenile writers popularizing wild animal lore. No

Boy Scout troop in Mt. Holly existed for him to join. As older men, his sons Henry Jr. and George Rhyne speculate that their father taught himself woodcraft.

However it was that Henry Rhyne managed to become such an accomplished woodsman, he started early. One formal family picture when he was a young boy shows him holding a slingshot. As a teenager, he purchased a black powder musket supposedly used in the Revolutionary Battle of Kings Mountain for twenty-five dollars, and it remained a prized possession for the rest of his life. As an adult, Henry Rhyne spoke to his sons about his boyhood hunting and fishing as if it had always been an essential part of his life. He almost seems to have been born with an attraction to wildness.

Rhyne's summers as a child in Blowing Rock started an enduring affinity for the North Carolina mountains. His grandfather Henkel, who owned a Statesville livery stable among several businesses, presented him with a new pony every summer in Blowing Rock, and there he learned to ride. Rhyne also went out in the woods gathering chestnuts and mushrooms. The latter activity proves that his lifelong enthusiasm for mushrooming began as a child. In the final decade of Rhyne's life, he recalled the lasting impression that the magnificent vistas down the Johns River Gorge and up to Grandfather Mountain made on him as a boy. As an adult, he owned two splendid natural properties in the mountains—one on the Green River in Henderson County and the other outside Triplett, near Boone in Watauga County—where he spent considerable time hunting, fishing, and mushrooming. His deep affection for these mountain parcels rivaled his feelings for the native lands of eastern Gaston County.

During the fifteen years after graduating from Mt. Holly High School, Henry Rhyne's outdoor activities disappeared and other priorities emerged. After graduating in the Davidson College Class of 1934, where he was a record-setting high jumper, and studying briefly at the University of Virginia, Rhyne returned to Mt. Holly and became a cotton broker. In 1936, he wed Eleanor Nelson from a well-to-do Englewood, New Jersey, family. Newlyweds Henry and Eleanor Rhyne moved into a new, fine brick starter home next to his parents. Their two sons, Henry Jr. and George Rhyne, were born exactly one year apart on August 18, 1937 and 1938, respectively.

In spite of two beautiful sons and so much else in their favor, Henry and Eleanor Rhyne's marriage was troubled irreparably and lasted only four years. When they divorced in late 1941, the boys went to live with their grandmother first in New Jersey and later Manhattan, and they visited their father regularly on holidays. For Henry Rhyne, the divorce returned him to his former status as a single man, and he remained so for the next thirty-four years. Through all these unmarried years, he had many girlfriends and at least one serious romance. His independence from many family obligations freed him to hunt and fish.

When the Japanese bombed Pearl Harbor in December 1941, Henry Henkel Rhyne enlisted as an American Airlines commercial pilot in the nation's Air Transport Command (ATC) that employed civilian pilots to fly air transportation as part of the larger war effort. Like many other well-to-do teenagers, he had learned to fly privately in high school and gained celestial navigation skills then or in college during a summer vacation spent boating in Florida. Rhyne flew for ATC until the war ended, when he retired from commercial aviation.

After the war, Rhyne returned to Mt. Holly first to briefly resume his career as a cotton broker. For the next three decades, he lived in his childhood home on North Main Street with his mother "Miss Alice" Rhyne. His parents had divorced some years earlier during the Depression, and father Henry A. Rhyne lived in an apartment above one of Mt. Holly's banks. Son Henry Rhyne also maintained his downtown office at the central intersection of Main Street and Charlotte Avenue, fully furnished with an upstairs apartment. This was the same office filled with sporting memorabilia that I visited in 1999.

Living with his mother, Henry Rhyne shared her comfortable lifestyle. Loyal and devoted servant Leo Pressley acted as cook, butler, and chauffeur for "Miss Alice," who operated one of Gaston County's most exclusive fine antique shops out of her home. Another local Black man, Torrence Moore, worked as a handyman and laborer for Henry Rhyne, his parents, and others in Mt. Holly (including my parents). Almost everyone in town liked Moore because of his outgoing, friendly personality, his enormous six-foot-nine height, and a nearly constant habit of singing popular tunes with his beautiful baritone voice. Henry Rhyne held typically conservative racial attitudes.

Sometime during the Truman administration, probably in 1946, Henry Rhyne and his father suffered devastating financial setbacks in their cotton brokerage business when federal regulators suddenly and unexpectedly imposed price controls on cotton commodities. As a result, Henry Henkel Rhyne abandoned the cotton business and supported himself with a variety of new ventures. He started a small loan company in Mt. Holly, later opening a second branch in

Newton, North Carolina. He purchased two farms near Mt. Holly, stocked with beef cattle. He bought and sold real estate. As a shrewd securities trader, he played the stock market successfully. Eventually, he also produced steady income streams from his fur trapping and Christmas trees harvested off his Green River property. All these endeavors brought Henry Rhyne financial security, partly because he lived on a tight budget but mostly because he was such a smart businessman. Family and friends might smile about Rhyne's frugality, but no one doubted his investment abilities.

Settled in Mt. Holly, Henry Rhyne resumed his life as an avid hunter, fisherman, and outdoorsman. During school and summer vacations with his oldest teenage son, who was also a sportsman, Rhyne frequently hunted and fished. Rhyne Jr. remembers bass fishing both above the Mountain Island Lake dam and in the South Fork of the Catawba River. His father fished from an Old Town canoe, using only bamboo fly rods and his own tied flies or homemade lures. Rhyne Sr. taught his son how to paddle and steer a canoe silently using the J-stroke on just one side. He also showed Rhyne Jr. how to make his own fishing lures: precisely placing the necessary hooks and spinners into plaster of paris molds and then pouring in molten lead. Once the lure cooled and hardened, Rhyne Sr. painted it with appropriate dots and bright colors to make an attractive artificial bait. Rhyne Jr. remembers regularly catching fish with his dad's homemade lures. In 1949, when the first mass-produced Zebco spinning reels hit the market, Rhyne Sr. refused to purchase one and stayed strictly a fly rod purist.

Son Henry Rhyne recalls one father-son hunt particularly well because they capsized their canoe in the

South Fork River during the dead of winter. During a vacation, the pair decided to float the river in a canoe to squirrel hunt. Driving separate vehicles, they parked son Rhyne's sporty Studebaker Commander Coupe downriver at a convenient spot to provide transportation when they finished, and then drove father Rhyne's car upstream to begin the hunt. The stretch of the South Fork they were on was swift and icy cold.

At first, all went well as they drifted along. Soon enough, Rhyne Sr. spotted a squirrel, shot it out of a tree, and it landed precariously on a steep, high bank. Concerned that the squirrel might roll down and sink into the river, Rhyne kept yelling at his son to keep his eye on the kill while he struggled to navigate the strong current and paddle to the bank. Things quickly went wrong. The canoe caught a stump sticking out of the riverbed, the boat flipped, and both hunters fell into the frigid water. Fortunately, they held on to their guns, and there was a close sandbar where they righted the canoe. Collecting themselves, they relaunched to the bank and finally grabbed the squirrel. Soaked to the bone and freezing cold, they still had to drift downriver some distance to make it to the Studebaker. When they arrived, the heater in the car didn't work, and the ride back was miserable. But they got their squirrel.

Henry Rhyne Jr., who met many crack shots in his years as an Air Force airman, contends that his father was the finest natural shot he ever saw. Several stories about his father's shooting make a strong case. According to Rhyne Jr., his father was such a deadly marksman with a .22 rifle that he consistently hit a squirrel moving up a tree in the head so as not to spoil the meat. Once while at home watching a Western movie on television in which a gunman/actor dramatically freed a person from a hangman's rope by shooting it in two, young Henry Rhyne declared such a feat impossible. His father disagreed and took a Benjamin .22-caliber pump-action air rifle into the front yard to prove it. There he picked out a walnut hanging from its stem about sixty feet away and fired a single shot trying to break the stem and drop the walnut. When the walnut did not fall to earth after the shot, young Rhyne thought his father missed. But he was wrong. When the two walked up to the walnut for a closer inspection, they saw that Rhyne Sr.'s center shot had left just enough fiber on each side of the pellet hole not to break the stem and leave the walnut hanging by threads. The shot was perfect. All these stories about Henry Rhyne's shooting ability are almost incredible but nonetheless absolutely true. He was a brilliant marksman.

Starting in the early 1950s, Henry Rhyne expanded his hunting to include big game: whitetail deer in North Carolina and moose in Canada. With no deer then in most of the North Carolina Piedmont, Rhyne traveled to the Uwharrie Mountains in the center of the state where whitetail had been successfully reintroduced. In late fall 1955, an early moose-hunting trip took him to the Lac Lacroix region of northern Quebec Province, just south of James Bay, where two Native Americans guided him. Much of their time was spent canoeing in a terrain that was "honeycombed with lakes," and even included a canoe chase after one moose. Rhyne killed "a big prize," which he had mounted in New York, and of which the newspaper noted he "was understandably proud." Four years later in another newspaper article, Rhyne again happily related that he "bagged three moose while on another three-week hunting trip" in British Columbia on which "he also did a great deal of fishing." Three of Rhyne's moose trophy mounts survive to this day in the home of his cousin Charles Rhyne who lives in Mableton, Georgia.

Rhyne also fished regularly throughout these years. In January 1955, he caught a huge longnose gar while angling for bass, presumably in the Tar River, and reported his unorthodox catch to a Rocky Mount newspaper in eastern North Carolina: "Only last week I foul hooked one in the tail. After about 30 minutes I got him up to the boat where I shot him. I had no way of weighing this critter but I believe he would weigh between 15 and 20 pounds. He was five feet six inches long as measured with a boat paddle." Established in 2009, the existing North Carolina state record for a longnose gar is four feet, five and half inches long and a weight of twenty-five pounds. Although his catch was unofficial, Rhyne's foul-caught fish was more than a foot longer than the current state record.

The next year in 1956, old Davidson College classmate Alex Schenck approached Rhyne about purchasing one-third interest in a beautiful 5200-acre property on the Green River in Henderson County, North Carolina, with Alex and his wife Laurie Schenck both as his separate, equal partners. Rhyne's decision to buy into the Green River property would be a source of endless pleasure for him through trout fishing and mushroom hunting. Rhyne and the Schencks employed a full-time caretaker to guard the property, and Rhyne eventually parked an Airstream trailer on the place to spend the night. In July of that year, Rhyne caught two seventeen-inch trout on a single cast. He was so proud of his feat that he shared the news with *The Charlotte Observer*. As with everything else Rhyne did outdoors, he excelled as a trout fisherman.

Because of Henry Rhyne's great mechanical aptitude, his determination to do everything himself (probably to save money), and his interest in Early and Native American material culture and folkways, he developed into a fine woodworker and carver, a basket maker, a photographer, a fair blacksmith and gunsmith, and an all-round handyman and craftsman. He became fascinated with and learned everything he could about primitive, traditional technologies of Native Americans and the frontiersmen. He taught himself how to start a fire seven ways without using a match or lighter. He made his own hominy grits out of wood ashes, brewed his own beer, and fermented his own wine. He operated his own dark room. As a single man, there were no boundaries between his domestic and outdoor life. Son Henry Rhyne Jr. remembers that in the early 1950s his dad's bedroom contained fly-tying materials and tools, gun cabinets, and equipment to load his own rifle and shotgun shells, which Henry Rhyne always did himself. Eventually his workshops and storage spaces grew into the garage's upper floor and basement (the blacksmith shop) and also his downtown office.

Through the years, Rhyne expanded his fine crafts to include homemade knives, a black-powder musket, split-oak baskets, ox yokes, totem poles, frog gigs, fishing lures, tied flies, and a bow and arrows to shoot fish. He also collected guns and probably owned more than a hundred in his life. He would buy Springfield .03s and Mauser .98s in large lots and improve or "sporterize" them for resale, keeping the best ones for himself. All these things were made or improved expertly. With the musket he built from a kit, he became well known locally as a black powder authority. His library was completely practical and included books on basket weaving and mushroom identification. He did everything to the highest standards, verging on perfectionism. He could not understand why everyone did not share his commitment to excellence. He truly may have been a polymath who could do or fix or make almost anything.

By the 1960s, Henry Henkel Rhyne's outdoor habits were well established and included hunting, fishing, mushrooming, trapping, and photography. In 1964, Sara Hodges, a local wild edibles expert living in adjoining Mecklenburg County, identified Henry Rhyne as a regional expert on morel mushrooms, always considered a special delicacy. In a *Charlotte Observer* article about her collecting, Hodges related that she was "trying to ferret out that information from Henry Rhyne of Mount Holly who knows a spot where they grow." Rhyne also developed an interest in another new outdoor activity. In the mid-1960s, he took up nature photography with his usual drive to excel and soon was winning awards in *Charlotte Observer* photography contests.

Trapping was another serious sideline that brought Henry Rhyne great pleasure and extra income. Rhyne set traps for muskrat, mink, and fox all over eastern Gaston County. According to fellow Gaston County master trapper and friend Bill Falls, Rhyne was the finest fox trapper he ever knew. In a single season, Rhyne trapped 100 muskrats for his cousin Charles Rhyne to make a fur blanket, picking out 40 pelts that matched perfectly in color. In the mid-1970s when Rhyne's friend Allein Stanley began mushrooming with him, he already knew in minute detail every creek bottom and stream in eastern Gaston County because of years spent trapping. Stanley claims that Rhyne was more a trapper than a hunter. His hunting buddies might have argued the opposite. Because he excelled at everything he undertook, it was hard to say exactly what Henry Rhyne did best.

In 1963, Henry Rhyne took at least two pleasure trips that exposed him to spectacular natural scenery and Native American history and culture: one a month-long visit to the Canadian Rockies and Alaska and the other to the Mayan Ruins at Chichén Itzá, Mexico. His trip to the Pacific Northwest began with visits to Victoria and Vancouver. Next he took an inland sea voyage to Ketchikan and then Skagway, Alaska. From there he traveled "by an old-fashioned railroad" to Whitehorse, then to Fairbanks where he flew to Anchorage before returning to Vancouver. Rhyne must have found the natural beauty, abundant wildlife, and Inuit culture awe inspiring. His visit to the Mayan Ruins also reflected his abiding interest in Native American cultures.

In late 1965, Henry Rhyne wrote famous Idaho outdoor writer Clyde Ormond two letters whose tone and contents indicate a well-formed friendship. How Rhyne and Ormond met is unknown, but they may have hunted big game together out West. Rhyne's first letter thanked Ormond for sending an autographed copy of his latest book, the outdoor classic *A Complete Guide to Outdoor Lore* (1964). All of Ormond's books, which included *Hunting in the Northwest* (1948), *Hunting Our Medium Size Game* (1956), *Hunting Our Biggest Game* (1956), and *Bear!* (1961), would have appealed strongly to Rhyne.

Rhyne's two newsy letters to Ormond also indicate the pace and intensity of his outdoor life. In late October or early November, he returned from a trip to the Copper River in southwestern Alaska, presumably salmon fishing. Back home the first week of November, he caught three black bass in one evening on his fly rod with a popping bug. The following Sunday he made a trip up to the Green River, where he caught two magnificent rainbow trout, one eighteen inches and the other twenty-one inches. On November 14, he headed to Virginia for the opening of deer season and killed "two nice Whitetail bucks. One was an eight pointer…and the other was a nice fat little spike buck just right for eating." Over the next month as waterfowl migrated south, Rhyne shot "his share of…mallards and blacks," and he did more successful fishing. He also received a letter of reply from famed Western hunting guide Erv Malnarich giving information about a hunting trip, probably for elk, that Henry Rhyne was considering the next fall in western Montana's Selway Wilderness. Henry Henkel Rhyne stayed constantly active outdoors.

In 1970, Henry Rhyne formed what became one of his two closest adult friendships with Robert "Bob" Holmes (b. 1935), who had moved two years earlier to Mt. Holly as Independence National Bank branch manager. Holmes, who had grown up in nearby Lowell and graduated from Western Carolina University, was thirty-five years old and twenty-four years younger than Rhyne. The two men were completely compatible and spent the next thirty years as inseparable hunting, fishing, and day-tripping buddies. As Holmes observed, "we had the same interests, same political views, and drunk [sic] the same liquor (Evan Williams bourbon)."

As constant companions, Henry Rhyne and Bob Holmes continued to do many of the same things outdoors Rhyne did previously. They hunted squirrels at the Sandy Ford farm outside Mt. Holly, fished for rainbow trout at the Green River, spent countless hours searching for mushrooms on Dutchmans Creek, and shot doves at lots of places around the Piedmont, including Bill Falls's popular annual dove shoot in nearby Bessemer City. After years of use, Rhyne's Winchester Model 12 automatic 12-gauge shotgun was well worn. It is interesting to note that with all the different kinds of game that Rhyne hunted during his life, he never hunted quail or owned or kept hunting dogs.

Rhyne and Holmes added several new pursuits to their outdoor repertoire. They hunted grouse occasionally on Rhyne's mountain property near Triplett, on foot without a dog, stopping intermittently to spook the big game birds into flight. They joined a deer and wild turkey hunting club that leased a big acreage outside Blackstock, South Carolina, sixty-three miles south of Mt. Holly, on the Chester and Fairfield county line. Often when hunting there, they spent several days camping at night in Rhyne's compact two-man trailer. They also frequently traveled to game lands that one of Holmes's cousins from Gastonia leased near Carlisle, Union County, South Carolina, about thirty miles from Blackstock, parking their trailer behind the property's hunting cabin. This part of the South Carolina Midlands held vast private and public timberlands that created prime deer and wild turkey habitat. In the 1970s, these hunting grounds were Gaston County's principal deer and turkey hunting destinations, and many other Gaston County deer hunters joined different clubs scattered across Chester, Fairfield, and Union counties.

When deer hunting in the South Carolina Midlands, Rhyne and Holmes used their self-climbing stands to climb into a tree each day before dawn and hunted until dark. They took breaks occasionally and ate a sandwich or a can of Vienna Sausages for lunch. Rhyne always shot a 30.06 rifle, and Holmes shot either a Savage Model 99 or a 250 Savage 3000. According to Holmes, "Henry killed more deer...because he was a whole lot better hunter. He knew the signs...where to go find them. He was just an excellent, excellent deer hunter." Holmes also was one of several friends who recognized Rhyne's encyclopedic knowledge of Southeastern flora and fauna. He observed that Rhyne "knew every shrub, every tree, every animal, and I guess every bug that walked. I had an uncle that was a botanist, and Henry, I think, knew more than he did."

According to Bob Holmes, Henry Rhyne was good company, had a great sense of humor, and sometimes "was a riot to be around." A serious practical joker, Rhyne once sent Holmes toward a particular Green River trout pool knowing that a large, harmless, nonvenomous water snake lived there. He was delighted when the snake surfaced and chased Holmes out of the water. At times, Rhyne was willing to invest considerable time and effort into playing tricks on his friends. On one such occasion, he put small Styrofoam spheres on toothpicks and secretly stuck them all over the yard of his neighbor, David Mason, who was also a mushroom enthusiast. Then Rhyne took his binoculars up to the second floor of his own house and enjoyed watching Mason's puzzlement as he inspected his *faux* fungi. Bob Holmes summarized his thirty-year friendship with Henry Henkel Rhyne with this simple, heartfelt tribute: "The best thing I can say about Henry is that he really made my life more enjoyable."

In 1974, Henry Rhyne started his second great adult friendship with Allein Stanley (b. 1927) through their shared passion for mushrooming. Stanley, a Statesville middle school science teacher, had joined the National Amateur

Mycology Association (NAMA) three years earlier in 1971, and she took the lead in organizing and hosting NAMA's first-ever annual foray (its most important annual membership meeting/outing) in the American South. The event was held that year in the North Carolina mountains at Camp Green Cove outside Tuxedo in Henderson County. Looking for additional properties nearby where NAMA attendees could hunt for mushrooms, Stanley contacted Henry Rhyne and Alex Schenck to ask if they would open their Green River property to NAMA members, which they did. This was the beginning of a close, loyal, lifelong relationship between Rhyne and Stanley, centering on their shared enthusiasm for mushrooms but deepening into a wonderful, devoted friendship.

In the beginning, Stanley and Rhyne may have been more or less equal in their mushroom knowledge, but not for long. Through NAMA's continuing education programs and Allein Stanley's own relentless quest, she rose quickly to become one of the nation's top amateur mycologists whose scientific knowledge and expertise were widely respected and sought out by amateurs and professionals alike. She also assumed a greater leadership role within NAMA and eventually was chosen as the organization's first female president in the late 1990s.

From the start of their friendship in 1974 until 2002 when Stanley herself moved to Gaston County, Rhyne and Stanley collected together often and established the following mushroom-hunting routine. Living in Statesville, Stanley frequently traveled forty miles to Mt. Holly and joined Rhyne for mushroom hikes in his home territory. Likewise, he often drove to Statesville, often first visiting his mother's grave there after her death in 1976, then meeting

Stanley to look for mushrooms somewhere she selected in Iredell County. Through the years, Rhyne also attended a few national forays with Stanley.

Even before meeting Allein Stanley, Rhyne's years in the woods allowed him to discover many choice mushroom spots in eastern Gaston County and on his two mountain properties. Both Stanley and Rhyne's cousin Charles Rhyne remember that one of Henry Rhyne's favorite and most productive sites was on the property of dentist Dr. Clyde McCall off the Stanley-Lucia Highway just outside the town of Stanley. Bob Holmes recalls a special place on Dutchmans Creek where morels grew. It is too bad that Henry Rhyne did not keep "a little black book" that revealed all his favorite mushroom-hunting locations. So much of what he knew has been lost.

Several years before the death of his mother "Miss Alice" Rhyne in 1976, Henry Rhyne married Barbara Ann "Bobbie" Seymour (1921–2001), originally from Martinsville, Virginia. Seymour attended Mary Washington University as a college-age student, had been married twice previously, and was living in Charlotte. Neither Henry's two sons nor his closest friends know much about their introduction and courtship. Bobbie Rhyne was a gracious, attractive-looking, traditional Southern lady, and not herself especially interested in outdoor life. But she accepted her husband's activities as a sportsman and woodsman. After the marriage, they continued to live in Miss Alice Rhyne's house on North Main Street in Mt. Holly. One of the necessary concessions was cleaning out Henry Rhyne's bedroom and moving the sporting equipment and outdoor supplies to the garage and his downtown office. Bobbie Rhyne often remarked that her husband's distracted driving was dangerous as he constantly craned toward the side windows to spot mushrooms. For twenty-five years of marriage until her death in 2001, Henry and Bobbie Rhyne stayed faithfully devoted to each other.

Throughout the 1980s, Henry Rhyne balanced his marriage, business affairs, and well-established outdoor recreations. Bob Holmes and Allein Stanley stayed his best friends and primary outdoor companions. Rhyne also made important land transactions involving his two mountain properties in Henderson and Watauga counties. In 1985, Rhyne and Alex and Laurie Schenck divided their Green River property after their long friendship ended bitterly. Rhyne received clear title to 1700 acres of the slightly more than 5200 acres that they originally owned jointly. Two years later on the Schencks' share of the property, son Alexander L. "Sandy" and daughter-in-law Missy Schenck opened a co-ed nature camp for young people that operates successfully to this day. Even after the property settlement, Henry Rhyne remained the sixth-largest landowner in Henderson County.

In 1987, through a complicated transaction involving Davidson College, Henry Rhyne sold his other mountain property outside Triplett to Eustace Conway, a twenty-seven-year-old, back-to-the-land, primitive-skills naturalist and educator then living in a teepee in Wilkes County. (Bob Holmes had already declined Rhyne's offer to sell the Triplett land to him at a favorable price.) Rhyne's fascinating relationship with Eustace Conway and his motives for selling the mountain land are two of the most enduring parts of his legacy. Conway became one the featured stars of the reality television show *Mountain Men* on the History Channel, and the property Rhyne sold is the core of

Conway's larger Turtle Island Preserve where the television series is filmed and broadcast. Through the television show, a national audience has learned about Rhyne's old mountain property.

Allein Stanley, who was then Conway's booking agent for speaking engagements mainly with area schoolchildren, introduced the two men. Even with Conway's extreme lifestyle, he and Rhyne had much in common and shared a deep affection for the outdoors and traditional cultures. Conway fell in love with the Triplett property and expressed a strong interest in purchasing it. Rhyne self-financed the bargain sale to Conway, almost certainly because he admired Conway's vision for the property as an educational center for nature and primitive/traditional cultures. Stanley believes that Eustace Conway was like "a son" to Rhyne, at least for a brief period of time before and after the land sale, and Rhyne was a significant influence on the young mountain man. If he were alive today, Henry Rhyne would admire what Eustace Conway has achieved at Turtle Island and take pride in what is happening on his old property.

In his eighties, Henry Henkel Rhyne stayed active outdoors and regularly went to his office to attend to business. In 1994 and 1995, he sold his Green River property to John A. Ball's family development company, Bear Wallow Interests, which developed about two-thirds of the property into luxury mountain homes on large lots and protected the rest through conservation easements. In 1996, Rhyne began attending annual regional forays at the Wildacres Retreat and Conference Center outside Spruce Pines, North Carolina, which Allein Stanley established after she became NAMA president.

During the final decade of his life, Rhyne also involved

himself with the American Chestnut Foundation's efforts to develop a blight-resistant strain and reintroduce the signature mountain tree species to its former range. Restoring American chestnuts obviously appealed to Henry Rhyne's childhood memories of Blowing Rock's magnificent chestnut forests. He even wrote an article published in *The American Chestnut Foundation* journal about his early years gathering chestnuts in Blowing Rock. Rhyne's interest in land conservation and chestnut restoration indicated his growing land conservation ethic and environmental awareness.

Henry Henkel Rhyne remained mentally sharp and physically active right up to the end of his life. He and Allein Stanley continued to gather mushrooms after he and his wife moved from his lifelong Mt. Holly residence to Gastonia's Covenant Village Retirement Community in the late 1990s. Rhyne discovered good mushroom habitat less than a mile away at the Gaston Memorial Park Cemetery. Bobbie Rhyne died in 2001, and Henry died two years later. They received Christian burials, and their graves lie close to Mt. Holly in a Mecklenburg County cemetery. At Rhyne's death, Bob Holmes wept for one of the few times in his life. One can only hope that mushrooms spring up profusely around Henry Rhyne's grave each fall.

What remains of Henry Henkel Rhyne's extraordinary outdoor legacy? His two Mt. Holly farms are heavily developed and bear little resemblance to the places he formerly loved. However, Eustace Conway's Turtle Island Preserve maintains his Triplett property in a pristine condition and perpetuates through its teaching programs and mission many of the values that Henry Rhyne shared. So does the *Mountain Men* television show, even if dramatizing Conway's lifestyle for reality television.

Henry Rhyne's Green River lands are mostly developed but partly protected through conservation easements and are connected to DuPont State Forest as a part of the magnificent "Blue Wall" conservation corridor that stretches across the North Carolina-South Carolina mountain border. The work of Sandy and Missy Schenck at their Green River Preserve introduces many young campers to the natural world that Rhyne cared about so deeply. All these protected lands he formerly owned and the ongoing, sympathetic missions of the Turtle Island and Green River preserves are fitting memorials to Henry Henkel Rhyne's love of nature.

Rhyne's wood carvings, split-oak baskets, guns, and homemade knives are scattered among his family and friends as treasured mementos of the man. All who knew and loved Henry Henkel Rhyne still smile whenever they speak of him. Only a fraction of the many stories about him have been gathered into this essay. He was an absolutely unforgettable, almost larger-than-life character.

Part businessman, part farmer, and part primitive woodsman, Henry Henkel Rhyne moved easily between high society, the business and investment worlds, and the great outdoors. But he was always happiest in the woods. Highly intelligent and absolutely original—some would say "eccentric"—Rhyne brought insatiable curiosity and great skill and energy to his time outdoors in eastern Gaston County, the North Carolina mountains, and the other places he visited. He mastered many of the skills and activities associated with field and fishing sports. He admired North America's indigenous people and, to a remarkable degree, gained the same intimacy with nature that they achieved so fully. He cultivated rich fellowship with other people who valued similar things. Henry Rhyne's exemplary life as a woodsman, sportsman, and naturalist, his detailed knowledge of local natural areas, and his powerful attraction to wildness still resonate powerfully with all who love and enjoy the natural world.

The sources for this essay fall into several categories. First are my series of interviews with all the following: Robert Holmes Interview, 21 November 2020; Allein Stanley Interview, 21 November 2020; George Rhyne Interview, 24 November 2020; Charles Rhyne Interview, 24 November 2020; and Henry H. Rhyne Jr. Interview, 28 December 2020. Newspaper articles can be found using Newspapers.com and the search terms "Henry Henkel Rhyne" and "Henry Rhyne," and limiting the search to the year or date of Henry Henkel Rhyne's life mentioned in the text. Other important sources are Henry Henkel Rhyne Sr., "Thoughts of Long Ago," *American Chestnut Foundation* 16 (Spring 2003): 20–21; and Henry Henkel Rhyne to Clyde Ormond, 8 November and 12 December, 1965, Clyde Ormond Papers, Special Collections, Brigham Young University-Idaho, Rexburg, Idaho. My visit to Mr. Rhyne's office is documented in my *Rankintown Notes: A Journal of Minding and Mending Family Land, 1991–2003* (Gastonia, NC: Richard Rankin, 2010), 93–95.

11

Life on the South Fork

Born in the depths of the Great Depression in the Art Cloth mill village between the town of Lowell and Spencer Mountain in North Carolina's southern Piedmont and raised there in a caring mill family, Bill Falls experienced an almost incomparable life outdoors. He grew up playing with friends along a three-mile stretch of the South Fork River and its feeder creeks. He learned from his father to hunt and fish. As a teenager, he trapped, shot, and sold wild game to mill village customers. When it came to the outdoors, Falls was a jack-of-all-trades. He was at ease paddling the river, trapping muskrats, catching catfish in wire baskets, shooting squirrels, setting rabbit boxes, hunting bobwhite quail and ducks, and gathering spring lizards to sell for fish bait. From Spencer Mountain down to Pinhook Island above McAdenville, no one was more at home in the woods or on the river. The great outdoors was his nursery.

The Art Cloth mill community really was "like a family," the title of the classic book on Southern mill village life. The National Weaving Company was the economic hub for the village's roughly 120 families who earned their livelihoods there. Father Glenn Falls worked as a loom fixer in the mill, and the family lived in one of the company's mill houses on Love Street. "The Front" was the village's small commercial district, consisting of three adjoining businesses: the grocery store, a grill, and the drug store. The latter also included a post office, pool room, and beer joint. Bill Falls, his three siblings, and other village children attended Art Cloth Grammar School from the first through eighth grades. Woodlawn Baptist Church was the village's social and religious center where the Fallses and other families worshiped. All the mill villagers knew and, for the most part, supported each other.

Dominated by Spencer Mountain just to the north, a 1250-foot Piedmont monadnock, the surrounding hillsides north and east of Art Cloth formed a rich, expansive wildwood that was the immediate watershed for the nearby South Fork River. The river itself flowed freely and contained occasional rapids on a three-mile stretch between Spencer Mountain's early twentieth-century hydroelectric dam and Pinhook Island's large rocky shoals and rapids. Bill Falls and his friends stayed on this section of the river.

With the village situated seventy-five feet above the river, neighborhood boys heard tree frogs singing outside their classrooms in springtime and anticipated warm weather. Always skinny-dipping, they swam in two swimming holes in Houser Creek (a small South Fork tributary toward Spencer Mountain). The larger one was called Rankin's and was located near Forney Rankin's farm across the river from the mill village. It had a high bank and was deep enough to dive into. The only problem was its popularity with rival boys from Lowell's Oakland Mill Village. Invariably, fights broke out between wet, naked boys. The Potts swimming hole was smaller and shallower, but safer because the Oakland boys knew nothing about it.

Right above the Potts pool was a popular fishing hole.

One of Falls's two best friends, Darrell Bumgardner, remembers spending "many happy hours" there catching white catfish and sun perch using a homemade fishing pole "with a cork from a shoe polish bottle and red worms that I dug up in our backyard." Falls, Bumgardner, and a third buddy, Harold "Sharpie" Wilson, ranged freely through the woods from the Spencer Mountain powerhouse to Pinhook Island, often camping out together. If they wanted to explore land across the river, they stripped naked, put their clothes in a bundle on their heads, waded across a shallow, and dressed again on the other side.

Like practically everyone else who worked in the mill, the Falls family had roots in the country, in their case nearby in Gaston County, and they brought rural folkways to Art Cloth. Father Glenn Falls came from a tenant farming family raised near Booger Mountain south of Gastonia. Mother Ethel Jenkins grew up on her family's dairy farm on Jenkins Dairy Road near Bessemer City where Falls's maternal grandparents continued to live and operate their dairy. Both grandfather Blaine Jenkins and father Glenn Falls were avid quail hunters. The strong family tradition of hunting, fishing, and woodcraft was especially valuable in young Bill Falls's training as an outdoorsman.

When Bill Falls was four years old in 1939, his father bought him a Remington .22 rifle for seven dollars at Ware Hardware in Gastonia, making layaway payments. More than eighty years later, Falls still owns the gun. His father taught him to shoot freestanding, without propping the rifle against anything for support. Shooting at a penny placed in the bark of a tree at thirty feet, Falls first learned to strike the tree and gradually improved until he could hit the penny with every shot. The next targets for shooting practice were wooden matchsticks at thirty feet. With practice, he became proficient at breaking them and, eventually, consistently lighting single match heads without snapping the stem. By the time Falls was eight years old, squirrels up a tree were easy marks.

In a landscape made up of small farms and woods, the Fallses bird hunted on the 500-acre Poston farm at the base of Spencer Mountain (now George Poston County Park), other adjacent farms, and Pharr Yarns properties on the river between Art Cloth and McAdenville. Glenn Falls always kept a bird dog. The first was a black-and-white or "rip rap" pointer named Joe. Next came Lady, a liver-and-white pointer. During bird season, Falls finished work at the mill at 3:00 pm, hurried home to change into hunting clothes, and walked into the field by 3:30 or 3:45 p.m. As a small boy of seven or eight, young Bill Falls trotted along to keep up with his dad. On Saturdays, they would drive to Grandfather Jenkins's farm near Bessemer City and bird hunt all day. None of these lands were posted, and they might find anywhere from two to five coveys in an afternoon. More on Saturdays at Jenkins Dairy. The best spots were thin woods and fields growing in broomstraw with lespedeza plots. Glenn Falls, who hunted with a 20-gauge Lefever double-barrel shotgun, emphasized hunter safety.

Until he was twelve-years old, Bill Falls was never allowed to carry a shotgun when he accompanied his father quail hunting. Instead, he carried the unloaded .22 rifle. His father kept the cartridges in case they saw a rabbit or squirrel for his son to shoot. As a boy himself, Glenn Falls had developed the ability to spot a rabbit sitting on its bed, and he told his young son that he would only let him shoot his .22 rifle while hunting when he could do the same thing. For several years as they hunted on foot, the youngster strained and scanned the ground without success. As an eight- or nine-year-old, he finally made good. Traveling on the River Road to bird hunt at the Poston farm, the pair had just crossed the Big Creek bridge. Father Glenn was about fifty yards ahead when son Bill yelled, "Here's a rabbit!" Racing back, Glenn Falls handed him a .22 cartridge and said, "Knock his eye out!" With a single shot, the proud youngster sent the rabbit tumbling out of its bed and down the bank. At last, Bill Falls was a hunter.

By the time Falls was nine or ten years old, he was ready to go hunting alone. Not long after shooting his first rabbit, he borrowed his father's shotgun to kill his first squirrel near Art Cloth. About three years later, as a twelve-year old, Falls went bird hunting on his own with his dog Lady. He was in the South Fork bottoms (currently Lowell's River Falls housing development) when she pointed. On the covey rise, he killed his first quail on his first shot. The beginner's luck did not last. As Falls recalls, "I had two pockets of shells, and I shot every one of them after that and never knocked a feather out."

At about the same age, Falls learned to catch rabbits in wooden boxes and muskrats in steel traps. His cousins, Joe and Jimmy Carpenter, who lived on Jenkins Dairy Road, taught him to build and set a rabbit box. Their father had a few muskrat traps. Soon Falls was catching rabbits in his boxes in the woods outside Art Cloth and setting traps for muskrats on the South Fork. He sold muskrat hides to Sears-Roebuck, which then included commercial fur buying among its many products and services. At twelve years of age, Bill Falls was a skilled rabbit and squirrel hunter, rabbit-box trapper, and an improving, novice muskrat trapper and quail hunter.

Even as a small boy, Bill Falls enjoyed earning money—in part to help support the family. As he notes, "I've always liked making money and don't care nothing about it when I get it." He earned his first, regular pay when he was four years old gathering chicken eggs from under a large Art Cloth boarding house. Mrs. J. O. "Bertie" Barr, the proprietor, paid little "Billy" to crawl into the open space under the house where the family's hens nested. He received four cents for a dishpan full of eggs and always spent his earnings right there at the boarding house where the Barrs sold soft drinks and candy bars. Egg money would buy an Orange Crush—the only soft drink his mother allowed him to drink—a Coke for his mother, and sometimes a candy bar to share with the family.

At twelve, Bill Falls started selling squirrels and rabbits in the Art Cloth village. Deadly accurate with his .22 rifle, he knew every den tree between Spencer Mountain and Pinhook Island. In season, often in the woods before dawn, Falls shot several squirrels before boarding the school bus at 7:30 am. Sometimes he took his .22 to school and stored it in the principal's office. After school, he retrieved the rifle, headed straight into the woods, and then squirrel hunted home. He was also catching a steady supply of rabbits in his boxes. One Christmas holiday as a fifteen- or sixteen-year-old, Falls caught thirteen rabbits in two weeks in boxes set at his grandfather's dairy farm. His customers paid him fifty cents for a squirrel and seventy-five cents for a rabbit. Some wanted the whole squirrel dressed because they ate the brains too. His meat business and muskrat pelts were providing him with steady income. By the time he was fourteen, Bill Falls was paying his own way in life.

The next phase in Bill Falls's life as a trapper came straight out of the South Fork River and was the result of his introduction to Lem Rhyne (b. 1886), a remarkable carpenter/woodsman then in his early sixties. Rhyne lived with his widower brother-in-law Colt Abernathy on Abernathy's farm across the river on Mountain View Street off Hickory Grove Road. He met Falls and his buddies while they roamed across the river through the woods on the Abernathy farm. Rhyne took an interest in them, and they called him "Pop." Rhyne possessed considerable wood lore, and among the many things he taught the boys was that pileated woodpeckers were known locally as "Indian hen woodpeckers." As a more experienced muskrat trapper, Rhyne showed Falls how to cure his muskrat hides by nailing them to a board. Lem Rhyne became Bill Falls's role model and mentor.

Without a boat of their own, the boys' access to the South Fork was limited to swimming and wading. But that was about to change. Darrell Bumgardner, Sharpie Wilson, and Falls were about thirteen or fourteen years old when they found a small boat "about the size of a box" abandoned in the river. The boat immediately broadened the range of their muskrat trapping. But when Lem Rhyne saw the dangerously dilapidated craft, he warned the boys, "You're gonna get drowned." Pop's warning came with a generous offer. He would build them a safe, sturdy boat at no charge if they would buy him materials. Thus began a project that transformed the scope and quality of their life on the river.

The boys' first challenge was scraping together enough money to buy boat lumber. Construction materials cost fourteen dollars. Bumgardner cut grass and sold picked blackberries to raise his share. With the necessary funds in hand, Lem Rhyne felt confident enough to go to Hawley Lumber in Stanley, eight miles away, and pick out boards to build a beautiful, solid boat. He chose twelve-inch planks for the walls, which he called "the gunnels," and tongue-and-groove boards for the bottom.

Picking up and delivering the lumber was another adventure. Bumgardner, who was a year older than Falls, still did not have his driver's license. But nobody cared that he used the Gilliam's Grocery truck, where he worked, to make store deliveries. So Bumgardner borrowed the store's Studebaker truck and drove with Falls to Hawley's Lumber to purchase and pick up boat lumber. They delivered it the same day to Pop Rhyne at the Abernathy farm.

Bill Falls will never forget watching Lem Rhyne, a master carpenter, at work building the boat. Rhyne's only tools were handsaws and a razor-sharp ax, employed like a drawing knife. The boat was thirty inches across and six inches deep in the front, forty-eight inches across and twelve inches deep at the center, and forty inches across and eight inches deep in the back. There were seat boards in the center and back. Bumgardner remembers it was fifteen feet long. Falls believes it was either fourteen or sixteen feet long. Whatever its actual length, this was a real boat, not a little box. The finished craft was built for work, but it was also a thing of beauty. According to Falls, "That sucker just scooted. It maneuverated real good" in the water. The new boat opened up the river to Bill Falls and his buddies. All points on the three-mile stretch between the Spencer Mountain powerhouse and Pinhook Island became easily accessible. With expert, hard paddling, Falls could even conquer the swiftest narrows in the river as he traveled upstream. Pinhook Island became his new, choice squirrel hunting ground.

By far, the most important new activity the boat made possible was trapping white catfish in wire-mesh baskets. Falls bought his fish baskets from Glen "Shorty" Long, who lived between Art Cloth and Lowell. Shorty Long himself basket-trapped in the nearby Catawba River, into which the South Fork flowed. He constructed his traps out of one-inch, mesh chicken wire and inserted an escape-proof entry funnel on one side. Then he dipped them in boiling tar as waterproofing and hung them on a post to dry for several weeks. With Pop Rhyne's newly built boat and Shorty Long's fish baskets, Bill Falls was ready to go into the catfish business. He set baskets up and down the river from Spencer Mountain to Pinhook Island, baiting them with cottonseed meal. Usually working alone, but sometimes with his father, it generally took about three days to accumulate a catch. Sometimes a single basket might contain only four or five catfish. Sometimes it might hold two hundred. On rare occasions, Falls and his father rolled full baskets too heavy to lift into the boat.

No one else catfished on the South Fork. Fifty years earlier, Pop's brother-in-law Colt Abernathy had sold fish that he netted on the river where it split at Pinhook Island. Abernathy caught mainly "redhorse fish," not catfish. Once an abundant, large Piedmont fish (adults averaging nine pounds in weight) that disappeared from North Carolina streams after the 1870s, robust redhorse preferred fast-flowing, rocky streams similar to the South Fork. It is entirely possible that as a young man, Colt Abernathy caught one of the last surviving populations of redhorses in Piedmont North Carolina. In the 1980s, a remnant redhorse fish population was discovered ninety miles east in the Pee

Dee River below Blewett Falls on the North Carolina-South Carolina state line.

Bill Falls peddled his new product line door-to-door and sold catfish all over Art Cloth. With an established clientele from his squirrel and rabbit business, he charged thirty cents per pound for dressed catfish. Because time was money, Falls became an expert at quickly dressing catfish—skinning, decapitating, gutting, and packaging his cleaned fish in wax paper. Dressed catfish were weighed on a set of vegetable scales. Some regular customers ordered a two-pound pack every week. At first, Falls only sold fresh fish. But as his business grew, his parents invested in a deep freezer to support their son's profitable enterprise.

Falls operated his South Fork catfish business successfully until his late twenties. In the ninth grade, he quit the football team and gave his newly purchased cleats to another freshman when the coach refused to let him leave practice early to get into the river. The boat that Pop Rhyne built for the boys was his mainstay and kept chained on the river behind his house. When Darrell Bumgardner joined the Navy at age seventeen, Falls inherited his share of the boat. Over the years, Falls claims he lost the boat fourteen times as others broke the chain, took a joy ride, and set it adrift after their fun. To recover his lost boat, he always "walked the riverbank" until he found it washed up downstream. More than once near Pinhook Island in the dead of winter, Falls stripped off his clothes, dove into frigid water, and swam 150 to 200 yards to retrieve his abandoned boat.

Spending so much time outdoors, Bill Falls discovered a number of special places. The old Miller Rhyne bottoms on Forney Rankin's land across the South Fork contained scattered old-growth trees left untimbered because they were hollow. As seen from the windows of the Art Cloth Grammar School, a single hickory tree in Rhyne bottoms towered above the rest. Falls eventually paddled over and found the giant, which was over a hundred feet tall and hollow for the trunk's first forty feet. He shot many squirrels out of this monarch of the woods. The wetlands around the Spencer Mountain powerhouse on the other side of the river were ideal waterfowl habitat, and Falls and his father occasionally shot ducks there. On the lower end of Pinhook Island was a large otter slide. A north-facing slope closer to the Falls home (today's River Falls subdivision) grew a dense stand of galax—a groundcover plant normally found in the mountains that flourished in small niche habitats on the South Fork. When Falls told one of his high school teachers about the galax patch, she related that as a child her family often gathered wild galax in Rutherford County, several counties farther west, to sell for Christmas wreaths.

At times, the woods could be a dangerous place. A pack of about thirty vicious wild dogs roamed between Spencer Mountain and McAdenville. Some were white-coated, and others looked like German shepherds. Their ears were pricked, and they carried their tails low to the ground. When Falls was a teenager, the pack once surrounded and chased him up a tree. Another time, one of the feral dogs caught in a muskrat trap snarled like a wolf. To protect himself, Falls carried his .22 rifle and shot wild dogs whenever possible. They were especially easy targets swimming across the river. His effort to eliminate them proved futile. The pack stayed large and healthy.

As a high school senior in 1955, Bill Falls embarked on his final business venture involving local wildlife. In this case, he was harvesting "spring lizards"—the local name for salamanders—from damp soil close to nearby small creeks or "branches." Throughout the Southeast in the 1950s, spring lizards were a premium live bait for the growing sport of largemouth bass fishing. Falls learned about spring lizards as bait from Jake McAllister, one of his Lowell High School teachers. Soon afterwards, Falls's uncle Gus Propst, a Gastonia policeman, informed his nephew that there was a strong market for spring lizards among Gastonia businessmen/bass fishermen. Without a local supply, fishermen drove to the North Carolina mountains to buy spring lizards for two dollars a half-dozen. In addition to the inconvenience of traveling so far to make the purchase, transporting mountain spring lizards to the lower-altitude, warmer Piedmont stressed and killed many. Falls sold local, healthy spring lizards reasonably priced.

Falls speculates that spring lizards were plentiful because Art Cloth residents dumped their trash and garbage into nearby creeks and branches, and salamanders came to eat earthworms attracted to rotting garbage. He used a minnow bucket, a bush ax, and a shovel to gather his live bait. After chopping away undergrowth, he shoveled up large chunks of damp soil to uncover the small amphibians. Broken glass in the trash and venomous copperhead snakes were the only dangers. Sometimes Falls gathered as many as twenty-two dozen spring lizards in an hour, often finding ten or twelve dozen within a thirty-foot stretch of ground. To package the live bait for sale, he placed each spring lizard in a moss-lined oyster cup purchased in bulk at Gastonia's Albion Wholesale Grocers. Then he perforated the lids with his pocket knife so the salamanders could breathe. His native spring lizards proved to be a hardy, attractive bait.

The high demand for spring lizards in Gastonia created a lucrative business. In his mid-twenties, working in the weaving plant and dye house of the Art Cloth mill, Falls made a dollar an hour and forty dollars a week. Pricing his spring lizards at two dollars and fifty cents per dozen, he could sell and deliver sixty dollars' worth of spring lizards in four hours. Falls drove his delivery route on Wednesdays, Fridays, and Saturdays and also made special deliveries on other days. As he recalls, "I had a regular lizard route, like a milk route."

Still living at home after graduating from Lowell High School, Falls took a succession of local jobs while continuing his side businesses selling catfish, rabbits, squirrels, muskrats, and spring lizards as well as bird hunting for sport with his father. His Carpenter relatives gave him the first steady employment in their landscaping business. After taking a mill job, Falls married Betty Hudson in 1956, and the young couple moved into their new mill house on Stowe Street. All the while, Bill Falls continued to earn extra income to support his new family through hunting and trapping.

Bill Falls finally stopped basket fishing the South Fork in his late twenties. After fourteen years of hard, steady use, Pop Rhyne's amazing boat finally wore out. In 1957, Falls took a job with an industrial sprinkler company in Charlotte, a line of work that he would build into a successful career. Sprinkler installations took him all over the Southeast and often away from home for days at a time. The changing nature of his work schedule competed with time spent in the woods. Even so, Falls maintained his spring lizard business into the mid-1960s. His remarkable life on the South Fork came to a close in 1968. That year, he purchased a farm outside Dallas, North Carolina, ten miles away, and moved his family there. The farm also became the headquarters for his industrial sprinkler company.

No contemporary individual lived on the South Fork River more fully—except perhaps Lem Rhyne—or drew greater sustenance and enjoyment from the wild than Bill Falls. For thirty years, he directly experienced the outdoors and used his hunting, fishing, and trapping skills to create profitable businesses and supply his mill village customers. All the while, Bill Falls moved seamlessly between Art Cloth and the South Fork River—with one foot in his Southern mill village and the other in wildwoods.

The sources for this essay are interviews with William Blaine Falls conducted by the author on 18 December 2016 and 17 October 2021, and Darrell Bumgardner, *A Place Called Art Cloth: Growing Up on a N.C. Mill Hill* (n.p., n.d.). A wonderful description of southern mill village life is provided in Jacquelyn Dowd Hall et al., *Like a Family: The Making of a Southern Cotton Mill World* (Chapel Hill, NC: University of North Carolina Press, 1987).

12

The Edge of Chicken Fighting

Although officially illegal in North Carolina, game chicken fighting has always been a popular rural pastime. Public opinion of the blood sport is complicated and mixed. Churchgoing people have long viewed the activity and its associated gambling as sinful. And animal rights activists have only added their moral outrage. Nevertheless, across the Southeast, many men still passionately practice the sport. Right now, less than two miles from my home at the old Rankin farm property on Stanley Creek, is a yard with more than seventy-five gamecocks in individual pens. If I go out in my front yard at dawn, I can hear them crowing in the distance. Those birds are bred and raised to fight.

While the activity is now a felony, authorities often look the other way to ignore chicken fighting. Although the fighting itself is unlawful, raising game chickens is legal. If the same inconsistent attitude existed toward marijuana, it would be alright to grow but not to smoke it. Why would anyone raise game roosters, which are stringy and tough to eat, unless to fight them? Deep down, the North Carolina legislature has always had mixed feelings about gamecock fighting. Local law enforcement shares the same forbearing attitude and only interferes in response to public complaints. Carried out in hiding to avoid arrest, chicken fighting is very much alive in North Carolina.

Gamecock fighting has an old, rich tradition in the immediate vicinity of Stanley Creek. In the early 1870s, less than five miles away on the west bank of the Catawba River, the Mountain Island Cotton Manufacturing Company was not only one of the area's earliest cotton mills but also became a regional center of game chicken fighting. Two older brothers, Ferdinand A. and Walter K. Tate, who owned the mill, and their teenage brother, Charles W. "Charley" Tate, all fought game chickens. Most of the factory's 200 mill hands raised gamecocks for the Tates. These workers lived around the mill on individual four-to-five-acre farming plots where each kept a small flock for their bosses. In chicken-fighting lingo, raising gamecocks for another owner is known as "walking" the birds. The saying, "the cock of the walk," comes from this activity.

Sometime between 1873 and 1875, one of Charley Tate's friends, Paul Barringer, visited Mountain Island to attend an upcoming chicken fight. A teenager from one of the area's most prominent Lincoln County families, Barringer studied "every part of the industry" during a weeklong stay and left a marvelous eyewitness account of the Tates' operation. Before the main event, he and Charley Tate drove a wagon around the surrounding mill neighborhood to pick up about thirty of the farmed-out fighting roosters. The most common local breeds were "White Pyles, Shawl-necks, Irish Grays, Flaery Eyes, and Warhorses." Barringer observed with fascination how these same gamecocks were housed in the mill's abandoned dyehouse, where they were carefully prepared for their upcoming matches. These practice sessions included sparring bouts between gamecocks wearing small "muffs" or tiny leather boxing gloves fitted over their spurs to prevent serious injuries.

The dyehouse also housed the large pit where the regional chicken fight or "main" was held between the Tates, other locals, and their opponents from Edgefield County, South Carolina. The contest attracted several hundred local spectators, the Edgefield contestants, and a handful of individuals from as far away as Virginia and Tennessee. Barringer estimated that total bets on the main approached $1,000, which would be the equivalent of over $25,000 today. There were seven matches between local and Edgefield cocks in the main contest. The South Carolinians won five and lost two. Although Barringer made no mention of other preliminary minor matches, known as "hacks," these were standard fare at all chicken fights and certainly also took place.

Barringer identified none of the Edgefield fighters at the Mountain Island event by name. The "main backer" was an anonymous "ex-Confederate general." Two other Edgefield sportsmen most likely in attendance were former Confederate officers Col. Thomas G. Bacon and his nephew, Maj. John Edmund Bacon. The Bacons were among South Carolina's greatest chicken fighters. Colonel Bacon developed the Gordon and Warhorse breeds of game chickens. In 1872, an Edgefield newspaper described Major Bacon as owning "the greatest coop of gamecocks in the country."

As the grandson of the Rev. Robert Hall Morrison, perhaps the state's most prominent Presbyterian clergyman and founder of Davidson College, young Paul Barringer had no difficulty setting aside his evangelical upbringing or respect for the law to enjoy the fighting festivities. Gamecocking was then classified as a misdemeanor. According to Barringer, the pursuit "sounds like a cruel and bloody sport, but we must remember that no cock in the history of the world was 'made to fight.' They fought because they loved it." Paul Barringer, the Tates, and their associates saw no moral dilemma in gamecocking and disregarded its unlawfulness. Chicken fighters included former high-ranking Confederate officers, pioneering textile manufacturers, and the grandson of Davidson College's founder.

The Tate family sold the Mountain Island factory to new Baltimore owners in 1884, and the fate of mill-sponsored chicken fighting became uncertain. While no specific record of gamecock fighting around Rankintown or the Stanley Creek area exists until the 1970s, the sport certainly persisted and remained enormously popular throughout the state and region. With the local tradition so well established in the area, gamecock fighting probably occurred in smaller, more impromptu matches. Because many such fights often took place in outdoor seclusion, they were known as "woods fights."

By the 1960s in the Southeast, chicken fighting had developed into a mature sport. Beginning in 1899, just over forty miles south of Rankintown in Gaffney, South Carolina, newspaper publisher Edward Hope DeCamp started *Grit and Steel Magazine*, which became the gamecocking industry's premier publication throughout the twentieth century. With an international circulation and reputation, not only did *Grit and Steel* cover the sport's news; it also advertised all the specialty supplies and equipment necessary for cockfighting.

The sport of chicken fighting offered a variety of

contests that became increasingly competitive as they advanced from local to regional levels. These ranged from more informal fights in clandestine wooded locations to highly organized, top-flight contests in established venues with large arenas to accommodate contestants and spectators. Mid-sized fights took place at Catawba, North Carolina, and Pageland, South Carolina. The biggest regional contests were held at the Del Rio Pit in Cocke County, Tennessee (near Newport), the Boxwood Pit near Danville, Virginia, and the Toccoa Pit in northeast Georgia.

In the mid- to late 1960s, my introduction to game chickens came through boyhood and teenage summers spent working on our family's cattle farm on Stanley Creek. For five straight summers, I spent weekdays with farm overseer John Odell Haggins (1921–2004) and his wife, homemaker Rozella Hicks Haggins (1911–1994). The Hagginses had no children, but at least one of their nephews, Frank Haggins (about five years older than me), often stayed with them during summers. My cousin Cree Rankin, who walked 200 yards up the hill from Willowside, also joined us every day. As I reflect on my time with the Hagginses, I realize what a major, positive influence they were on me, especially Mr. Haggins. Extremely kind and patient with lively, inquisitive young boys, there was something mysterious about John Haggins, but in an absolutely benevolent way. He never swore and refrained from saying anything off-color or making derogatory comments about others. Although he led a modest life and never was able to turn a profit in our cattle business, he struck me during my teenage years as unusually noble and decent. Fifty years later, with a lifetime of relationships for comparison, he still does.

While the Hagginses were not openly affectionate with

each other, there was a quiet tenderness about their marriage. One of the compromises they reached was over game chickens. A fighter earlier in his life, Mr. Haggins had given up the sport because Mrs. Haggins considered it sinful. However, she did allow him to raise game chickens for other people and to subscribe to *Grit and Steel Magazine*. When not working, Mr. Haggins was an avid reader. Sitting in his reading chair in the den, he wore half horn-rimmed glasses and projected a serious, scholarly attitude. He mostly read two things, and he read them a lot: the King James Version of the Bible and *Grit and Steel Magazine*.

Mr. Haggins kept individual cages for roosters and several larger coops for hens behind the barn, down a hill, and out of sight. During the first few years, I suspect he had no more than thirty birds, including both sexes. But the number grew and must have approached fifty roosters by my last year. He never spoke of fights, but nephew Frank Haggins did often, and the sport always felt close by. Only once do I remember Mr. Haggins sparring two roosters behind the barn. He fitted the cocks with exquisite tiny leather sparring gloves over their spurs. The male fowls purely hated each other and attacked with incredible viciousness, wings flapping and gloved spurs flying. For a teenage spectator, it was absolutely thrilling to watch. If there had been blood and death—which there wasn't—I don't know if I would have enjoyed it. But, under the circumstances with the protective gear, I could have watched roosters fight all day long. We probably sparred the cocks for less than five minutes.

Toward the end of my years with the Hagginses, I became smitten with game chickens and wanted a hen of my own so that I could raise them. There was one particularly good-looking hen that I admired, and Mr. Haggins was willing to give her to me. But somehow, it never happened. Perhaps Mr. Haggins asked my father, who probably rejected the idea as a gateway to vice. After getting my driver's license, I quit working at the farm and found other paying summer jobs. My attention switched to participating in team athletics and a first girlfriend, and my brief fascination with game chickens receded. After all these years, I have still never attended a cockfight.

My interest in chicken fighting has returned in the last few years. A new friendship with a colleague's father, Richard Paxton, provided new access to the sport. From the 1970s to the 1990s, Paxton lived in Mecklenburg County and was a serious chicken fighter. Gene Pillow, whose family ran Pillow's Store near the Rankin farm, provided more information. Pillow also fought chickens, and he paid John Haggins to walk birds for him.

Both Richard Paxton and Gene Pillow remember local cockfighting during the 1970s and 1980s. Pillow and another longtime Stanley Creek neighbor told me that regular woods fights occurred at the Old Wyatt place off the Lowland Dairy Road. But an even bigger and better organized indoor fighting pit was located several hundred yards behind Pillow's Store at the intersection of Old NC Highway 27 and the Lowland Dairy Road. William "Flattop" Lambert owned and operated it, and both Paxton and Pillow went to fights there. Frank Haggins probably did too.

Flattop Lambert's fighting pit is a matter of public record because the police raided it at 11:30 am on Sunday, June 12, 1983. Responding to local tips, the Gaston County Police were surprised to find 300 people in attendance. Off to the side of the pit, there was a wheelbarrow full of dead roosters. While two uniformed officers waited a short distance away in their patrol cars, three plain-clothed, undercover agents made their way pit side just as two participants ran in and announced "the police are here." Pandemonium ensued, and the crowd literally knocked down the building's temporary siding in the rush to escape.

With chicken fighting then a misdemeanor, the five police officers arrested Lambert and issued citations to another thirty-one fighters. One man from Alabama received a citation, two from South Carolina, and the rest from Gaston and adjoining Mecklenburg and Cleveland counties. All others fled the scene. One heavy-set fugitive became the butt of local jokes when he fell into a gully behind the pit building and was unable to climb out on his own power. Father Russell and son Gene Pillow, who drove their golf cart to the fights from nearby residences, returned home without incident.

Stories of local cockfighting not only revive past memories of the farm but also rekindle my current interest in the sport. Although part of me wants to attend my first chicken fight, I doubt I ever will. If the cocks all wore sparring muffs and protective headgear, then I would be on the front row. But, in such circumstances, would there ever be a victor? There is also the risk of arrest.

Amid the undeniable cruelty of violent blood sports, there is also an undeniable beauty in wildness. In James Dickey's poem "The Heaven of Animals," the famous poet imagines an eternity in which predator and prey ceaselessly complete the cycle of stalking, pouncing, killing, and then miraculously springing back to life:

At the cycle's center,
They tremble, they walk
Under the tree,
They fall, they are torn,
They rise, they walk again.

Unfortunately, here on earth, when gamecocks kill each other, they neither "rise" nor "walk again." The wheelbarrow at Flattop Lambert's was full of dead roosters. That is an unavoidable, brutal truth.

When dawn arrives at Willow Hill and I hear my neighbor's gamecocks crowing, I can't help but recall happy summers with the Hagginses. Their former house sits less than 600 yards away from where I now live. With all the sport's moral contradictions and bloodlust, hearing the roosters reminds me of the excitement of being around game chickens. Is it possible that somewhere in heaven John Haggins is taking turns reading his Bible and old copies of *Grit and Steel*? And James Dickey is watching dead gamecocks brought back to life to fight again? How wildness occurs in the afterlife remains a mystery. But imagining a perfect paradise without it is nearly impossible.

James Dickey, "The Heaven of Animals," in *The Whole Motion: Collected Poems, 1945–1962* (Wesleyan University Press, 1992).
For the account of olden-day chicken fighting at the Tate Cotton Mill, see Paul B. Barringer, *The Natural Bent: The Memoirs of Dr. Paul B. Barringer* (Chapel Hill: University of North Carolina Press, 1949), 168–74.

13

Stewarding the Stanley Creek Forest in an Imperiled World

The prehistoric forest that preceded Twin Brooks and Stanley Creek forests in eastern Gaston County of the North Carolina Piedmont must have been truly magnificent. The two forests were originally continuous, and their watersheds drained into creeks that were tributaries of larger Dutchmans Creek, which flows four miles into the Catawba River at Mt. Holly. Twin Brooks sat on lower slopes and lowlands south of South Stanley Creek. The Stanley Creek Forest occupied the ridgeline, high hills, ravines, coves, and lowlands between South Stanley and Stanley creeks and, in a few places, crossed beyond the latter. Probably by 1840, settlers had already girdled, timbered, or cleared most of these virgin woodlands, and second growth returned. My great-grandfather Col. Richard Rankin (1804–1899), who lived at nearby Willowside farm, owned the young, recovering forest.

The few giant trees surviving from the older forest suggest its awesome original character. One white oak and another post oak on my property are over four feet in diameter at breast height, roughly one hundred feet tall, and have large canopies. There is a great hickory just west of Willowside Drive that is nearly four feet in diameter and over one hundred feet tall. At least two other ancient trees now gone have left impressive records. Located at the old

James C. Rankin house site, the Rankin Oak was listed in *Trees of the Southeastern States* (second edition) as the largest red oak in the entire Southeastern region. By the early 1930s, the Rankin Oak was 5'6" at breast height, probably about 75 feet tall, and had an enormous 123-foot canopy spread. With its huge girth, relatively short height, and sprawling branches, the Rankin Oak's contour resembled a southern live oak more than it did the tall, stately white oaks and hickories that dominated the surrounding Piedmont woods. In 1877, Col. Richard Rankin cut down a water oak on his property that was described as a "monster tree." The water oak was 160 years old and 4'9" at the stump. With 20 feet of huge trunk still lying uncut on the ground, the single tree had already produced 6,500 shingles, 150 rails, and 50 loads of wood. Once upon a time, such giant trees must have been commonplace in the old-growth woods.

Col. Rankin bequeathed or sold the woodlands that would become the Twin Brooks and Stanley Creek forests to his heirs, who cleared large, scattered agricultural fields. These croplands lay mainly on either side of the road that ran through the woods on its way from Mt. Holly to Stanley. The steep slopes and ravines of the forest made much of the property impractical to farm, thus safeguarding the maturing, hilly woodlands.

By the mid-twentieth century, one line of Col. Richard Rankin's heirs sold several hundred acres of their property to outside owners, of which the seventy-acre Twin Brooks woodland was a parcel. Another line of Col. Rankin's descendants kept ownership of just over 500 acres that would become the bulk of the Stanley Creek Forest. A third branch (my direct ancestors) owned another 150 acres that would become smaller additions to the forest. For perhaps 200 years, big sections of these forestlands grew largely undisturbed. The exceptional quality of the second-growth woods was more evidence of just how fantastic the ancient forest must have been.

In 1999, a team of field biologists surveyed both the Twin Brooks and Stanley Creek forests as part of the broader *Gaston County Natural Heritage Inventory* (hereinafter cited as the *Inventory*) and designated them as official "natural heritage" sites because of their exceptional quality. The Twin Brooks property was graded as regionally significant, meaning that it was one of the best remaining forests in Gaston County and the three surrounding North Carolina counties to north, east, and west (York County, South Carolina, on Gaston County's southern border, and therefore out of state, was exempted from the survey). The Stanley Creek Forest was given a higher status and judged to be one of the finest natural heritage sites in the entire state.

While the "natural heritage" designation gave no permanent protection to named properties, the state-level status did offer the possibility of state conservation funding through a competitive grant process. The State of North Carolina created a mitigation fund, called the Ecosystem Enhancement Fund (EEF), to offset state road construction that destroyed any state-level natural heritage sites. When such losses happened, EEF purchased and permanently conserved a comparable, unprotected natural heritage property somewhere else in North Carolina. Only state-level sites (like the Stanley Creek Forest) qualified for EEF dollars. Regional natural heritage sites (like the Twin Brooks Forest) did not. The Ecosystem Enhancement Fund would ultimately save the Stanley Creek Forest.

Against a backdrop of metropolitan Charlotte's

explosive growth, the different fates of the Twin Brooks and Stanley Creek forests represent extremes in conservation failure and success. Despite repeated efforts to save the Twin Brooks property in the years after 2000, first an industrial park and then a large tract home development obliterated and replaced it. Lack of conservation funding caused this defeat. The tragic loss deprives present and future generations of a regional natural treasure. Living now less than two miles away and growing up only a few miles farther, I never hiked Twin Brooks nor experienced it myself, though I drove by it countless times without suspecting how special it was. Other than the field biologists who surveyed the woodlands for the *Inventory*, there are few people, if any, who remember what it was like. Not even photographs survive. It has vanished. The *Inventory* description remains a haunting reminder of all that was lost. Twin Brooks was notable not so much for the size or age of its trees, shrubs, and herbs but for its tremendous plant diversity. This diversity resulted from the underlying soil's basic pH— uncommon in Piedmont North Carolina—which produced an uncharacteristically rich type of plant community known as a Basic Mesic Forest.

One species in Twin Brooks, the bigleaf magnolia, was a genuinely rare understory tree with North America's largest deciduous leaf, which can attain a length of three feet. It grows naturally nowhere in the eastern United States except Gaston County and four other contiguous counties, where it is locally common in certain places. The rarity of bigleaf, its spectacularly large leaf, and its beautiful flower make it a charismatic signature species. Because of the size of its leaves, bigleafs are wonders to behold in the woods, and young children around Stanley call them "elephant ears."

The presence of bigleaf made the Twin Brooks Natural Heritage Site even more special. All of this disappeared when the forest was destroyed. The "natural heritage" status provided no legal protection whatsoever against development.

Unlike Twin Brooks, the Stanley Creek Forest became a conservation victory. At first in 1999, *Inventory* field biologists focused on an approximately 150-acre core within the almost 600-acre area that would become the Stanley Creek Forest. Inside this 150-acre core area, the biologists identified three particularly rich sites. One of these was a 28-acre "steep-sided cove" that included "hundreds" of bigleaf magnolias, including many with trunks 6 inches or greater in diameter, which is exceedingly large for the small understory tree. In the absence of any other natural heritage sites in Gaston County with a similarly outstanding stand of bigleafs, and with Gaston and four nearby counties containing the only native bigleafs east of the Mississippi River Valley, the Stanley Creek Forest's bigleaf stand may be the finest in the eastern United States. As someone who lives in and whose ancestors once owned the Stanley Creek Forest, I can be accused of bias. But the *Inventory* supports my claim.

More than just bigleaf magnolia trees make the Stanley Creek Forest so enchanting and sublime. Hardwoods more than three feet in diameter are scattered throughout the property. Uncommon in the Piedmont, mountain laurels grow on some of the steep slopes in the three core sites. Perennial wildflowers not only consist of Catesby's trilliums, native to the Piedmont's richest woods, but also a disjunct population of nodding trillium that are usually found only in the mountains. Other truly rare or uncommon Piedmont wildflowers and plants such as yellow lady slippers, ginseng, and wild cucumber are also present. Large boulders line the wet-weather creek beds that drain the coves. Visiting the most pristine sections of the Stanley Creek Forest in springtime really is—in the truest sense of the word—a *wonderful* experience.

After their initial study of the core area, *Inventory* biologists expanded their survey into the rest of the forest. There they realized the remarkable natural character of the whole 600-plus acres. In particular, rich bluffs along the entire length of the property grew scattered populations of yellow lady slippers and other threatened plants. The size of the forest also is distinguishing. For Piedmont North Carolina, it is highly unusual to have more than 600 acres of unbroken, mature forest. The *Inventory* designation made it official: the Stanley Creek Forest is a state natural treasure.

As I have written about elsewhere in greater detail, under the leadership of Catawba Lands Conservancy Director Ron Altman and Associate Director Sonia Perillo, the conservancy took the lead in the daunting challenge of securing a $3.2 million grant from EEF and negotiating a purchase from Rankin heirs who owned the 500-acre forest. North Carolina Senator David Hoyle (Gaston County) was instrumental in supplying political clout. After closing the deal, the conservancy named the property the Stanley Creek Forest. About 80 acres of woodlands that I owned and already protected through a conservation easement also were part of the original area first surveyed in the *Inventory*. Three other adjoining landowners added their conserved woodlands to the greater forest. The whole, continuous tract grew to more than 700 acres and became part of a larger 1200-plus-acre district known as the Stanley Creek Forest

Conservation Area. So it remains today. Creating the Stanley Creek Forest Conservation Area is one of the Catawba Lands Conservancy's greatest conservation triumphs.

Protected from all future development under current North Carolina laws, the Stanley Creek Forest nevertheless faces a host of threats to its environmental health and integrity. These include erosion, invasive species, tree blights and pests, urban encroachment, forest fires, extreme weather, and climate change. Stewarding the forest requires responding appropriately to the different threats, which range from local to global. Erosion control and invasive plant species are the most immediately remedial. Filling or covering eroded places with vegetative matter promotes revegetation. Invasive shrubs like autumn and Russian olive can be eradicated either using a specialized uprooting tool or a herbicide. Kudzu also can be eliminated where it takes root. Both erosion and invasive-species control lend themselves to volunteer efforts in the forest.

Other threats are far more insidious. The globalization of trade has introduced foreign blights and pests to native plants and trees. The Stanley Creek Forest once contained scattered chestnut trees that an early twentieth-century blight killed. Dutch elm disease and emerald ash borer beetles are attacking two other native species. In all likelihood in the future, other diseases and pests will afflict more plants. Tract-housing developments are springing up all around the forest. Especially to the south, undeveloped natural areas on South Stanley Creek are gone. There are promising conservation opportunities up Stanley Creek, and the Catawba Lands Conservancy and the town of Stanley would do well to focus their conservation energies there. If not, the Stanley Creek Forest Natural Area will eventually become a natural island within a sea of residential development.

More than any other existential menace, the specter of climate change looms over the Stanley Creek Forest. Warming temperatures hatch more frequent and powerful storms, especially hurricanes. In September 1989, Hurricane Hugo directly hit the Stanley Creek Forest, toppling trees extensively. Recently, Hurricane Ian lost most of its destructive force before it also came through. We are entering an era when storm damage to the forest is intensifying. There have been two fires set in the forest during my lifetime. In the late 1960s, one burned perhaps 50 acres in the forest's eastern side. About 25 years ago, an arsonist started a fire that burned about 20 acres within 500 yards of my home in the center of the forest. Climate change is only increasing the likelihood of forest fires as it brings more extreme weather, including periods of prolonged drought.

Longer-term rising temperatures also are altering species composition in the forest. Mountain species at home in cooler niche habitats face increasing stress or local extinction. In contrast, warmer-weather plants may find the forest more hospitable. The speed with which global temperatures are rising makes it difficult to predict overall damage to the forest. The apocalyptic magnitude of global warming requires resisting despair and mustering the political will at both national and international levels to solve the calamity. Each of us has a responsibility to vote for those who will work to reverse climate change and to accept our own role as fossil-fuel consumers in the global environmental crisis we face.

The Stanley Creek Forest is imperiled. The good news is that the splendid forest survives at all and is well worth saving. As agents in creation, we are called to sustain the natural world. For me, as a member of the family that once owned the forest for several generations and lives in it myself today, I feel a special responsibility of care. Faith, hope, affection, and gratitude inform my stewardship. But so does a deep conviction that stewarding the Stanley Creek Forest is only a local expression of a global environmental imperative on which the survival of the planet depends. Act locally, think globally, and pray ceaselessly for the creation.

For a more detailed account of the successful effort to acquire the Stanley Creek Forest Conservation Area, see my "Adventures in Land Conservation," in *The Margins of a Greater Wildness*, 12–30. For more about bigleaf magnolias, see my "The Rediscovery of Bigleaf Magnolias," in *The Margins of a Greater Wildness*, 74–83. See also Alan May, *Natural Heritage Inventory of Gaston County, N.C.* (Gaston County Quality of Natural Resources Commission et al., 2000).

14

Black Bears Rewilding the Stanley Creek Forest

Nobody knows for sure how long a breeding population of black bears has been gone from Gaston County. Bounties were paid for panthers and wolves killed in Tryon County and its successor Lincoln County (from which Gaston County was formed in 1846) until the mid-1780s. Surely a landscape wild enough to support panthers and wolves also retained bears. But at some indeterminate point in the past—perhaps 1800 is a good educated guess—native black bears disappeared not only from this immediate area but also from the rest of the Piedmont and, eventually, much of North Carolina. The bruin population clung to life only in the wildest margins of the state: the mountains and the swampiest parts of the coastal plain.

In the 1930s and 1940s, the creation of the Great Smoky Mountains National Park—a 522,000-acre preserve in the heart of the Smoky Mountains on the North Carolina-Tennessee border—and several national forests located in both the mountains and coastal plain guaranteed that breeding black bear populations would always survive in these sanctuaries. But in the rest of the state, bear numbers shrank and became limited to increasingly fragmented pockets of mountain and coastal wilderness. During my boyhood years of the 1960s and 1970s in Mt. Holly in the southwestern Piedmont, young transient male bears would rarely follow the Catawba River corridor down from the mountains and briefly be spotted near town, causing fleeting excitement before quickly retreating to higher country. The idea of bears repopulating the Piedmont seemed far-fetched. By the 1960s, state wildlife biologists shared a general concern that black bears would ultimately disappear entirely from the state outside Great Smoky Mountains National Park, our national forests, and a few other wild enclaves. The outlook for bears in North Carolina was bleak.

In response to declining numbers, in 1971 the North Carolina Wildlife Resources Commission established twenty-eight bear sanctuaries scattered throughout the mountains and coastal plain. The idea was to create core areas where protected populations could breed and expand outward. The bear sanctuary program succeeded beyond all expectations, proving to be one of North America's great wildlife management triumphs. With these sanctuaries as nurseries, the bear population began almost immediately to grow and spread toward the center of the state from the two established populations in the mountains and on the coast.

In the late 1970s, I witnessed the process of long-absent bears reclaiming former range in southeastern North Carolina near Council, Bladen County, on Neisler family private game lands where I deer hunted. Prior to then, bears had been missing for decades, but the sanctuary program brought them back. Now black bears are abundant throughout much of the coastal plain. Once while I was driving to Wilmington in the late 1990s, two large cubs ran fast across US Highway 74 in broad, open daylight. Never having seen bears in the wild, at first I thought they were a pair of black Labrador retrievers. The experience was thrilling when the young bears finally ran close enough to identify.

Over the last four decades, the two separate bear populations—mountain and coastal—steadily crept toward the center of the state (the Piedmont). This bear expansion can easily be tracked virtually because of an information-rich, color-coded map on the Wildlife Resources Commission's black bear website. With Gaston County located on the southwestern edge of the Piedmont, the growing mountain bear population is the one relevant to this area, as bears steadily occupy new lands to the east, moving closer and closer. This proliferation has been most dramatic since 2001. Before then, a breeding population was absent not only in Cleveland County to our immediate west but also in Rutherford and Polk, the two counties farther west toward the mountains. By 2010, bears were breeding all over Polk, Rutherford, and Cleveland, right up to Gaston County's western edge and clearly heading this way. Whether they would tolerate Gaston County's scattered natural areas in an otherwise heavily developed and industrialized landscape remained uncertain.

Unlike deer and wild turkey recovery efforts in which state biologists trapped and relocated wild animals as a way of reintroducing them into uninhabited areas, black bears are forced to expand on their own. Public fear of bears is so strong—even if unrealistic—that local folks reject any organized reintroduction. Beyond the bear sanctuary program and existing hunting regulations—which are all still in place—Piedmont bears must survive without any additional assistance from state wildlife biologists. The Wildlife Resources Commission even allows hunting in the people-filled Piedmont to keep out dispersing bears. Nevertheless, the bruins are winning in many places and are now present in Cleveland County, twenty miles to the west.

About three years ago in 2014, I began wondering if bears might return to the Stanley Creek Forest in northeastern Gaston County where my family has lived for generations. Fox hunting with older hunters near Waco, on the eastern side of Cleveland County near the western Gaston County line, my buddies told me that a black bear was living inside a nearby fox-hunting pen (a manmade, fenced enclosure of perhaps fifty acres constructed to let hounds run safely away from cars). According to the Waco fox hunters, this local bear came and went freely but preferred staying mostly inside the pen. What was stopping a bear in Waco from crossing the Gaston County line only a few miles away? Nothing at all.

About the same time, while I was driving to a Catawba Lands Conservancy property near Crowders Mountain State Park in the extreme southwestern corner of Gaston County, a large black bear foraged one early afternoon in a field outside the park. There were at least five other cars stopped to watch the massive beast, which must have weighed 350 pounds. During the same time frame, rumors circulated that a mother bear and her two cubs had been spotted near Blacksburg, South Carolina, not too far from Crowders Mountain State Park. If true, these reports were highly significant. A mother with cubs proved that a breeding population was establishing itself on Gaston County's southwestern edge.

All these sightings, however, were a good twenty miles away from Stanley Creek, and there was no bear population inside Gaston County's western fringe. Would black bears ever repopulate the Stanley Creek Forest and, if so, in how many years? Was it reasonable or ridiculous to hope? On the encouraging side, Stanley Creek did seem like an inviting place for a black bear. The Catawba Lands Conservancy already protected more than 1200 acres along the creek, and part of this land—including some of my own property—was designated as a state-level natural area because of the quality of its habitat. Wild turkeys, wildcats, raccoons, red and gray foxes, coyotes, deer, beaver, river otters, pileated woodpeckers, ospreys, and bald eagles already live in the forest. Large stretches along Stanley Creek are dense, thick, wild places that look perfect for a bear. Expanses of mature second-growth forest, full of acorn-bearing oak trees, occupy much of the nature preserve. The Stanley Creek Forest sure looked like a place where a bear could be fat and happy.

Whether the Stanley Creek Forest was a spacious enough wildlife sanctuary to host black bears was the open question. In places like Asheville, North Carolina, and Pittsburgh, Pennsylvania, bears demonstrate great adaptability and frequently make their dens inside city limits. In both places, however, mountain wilderness is close by. Not so in the Stanley Creek Forest. Also, there was the problem of poachers already killing wild turkeys and spotlighting deer in the forest. Would local folks tolerate black bears? Why was I even worried about the possibility? No bear had been seen anywhere near Stanley Creek for more than 200 years.

About 2015, I bought Mary Oliver's poetry book, *The Truro Bear and Other Adventures*. The title poem is about a mythical black bear that Oliver imagines living undetected in the local Truro Woods despite absolutely no evidence or indication of its existence there. The Truro bear was a phantom that satisfied the poet's longing for wildness. Reading the poem, I identified with the desire for the immediate wildness of a black bear. But the poem also brought a sad realization. Bears were no more inhabiting the Stanley Creek Forest than they were the Truro Woods. Even if the Wildlife Resources Commission map indicated an expanding black bear range, the relentless development radiating from Charlotte further degraded and fragmented suitable habitat. And there were no wilderness sanctuaries near the Stanley Creek Forest as in Asheville or Pittsburgh.

This was how things stood until 9:54 am on September 12, 2017, when Sharon Wilson, Catawba Lands Conservancy Land Stewardship Director, sent an email alerting me to the presence of a black bear. Tex Squires, a volunteer who monitors and polices the Stanley Creek Forest for the conservancy, had spotted a juvenile black bear in woods near my home. Both Wilson and Squires were completely reliable sources. There could be no doubt about their report, although they did not know the sex of the bear or its exact size. Wilson commented in her email, "I hope s/he does not get shot during hunting season. I hope you get to see it!" Fearing that any publicity might bring out potential bear killers, I told absolutely no one except my wife. It was hard not to share such exciting news. However, I did start driving home from work a longer way through the Stanley Creek Forest each evening, hoping to see the bear. But without any luck.

A week and a half after receiving Wilson's email, Federal Judge Craig Whitley, my friend who lives about four miles up Stanley Creek, sat next to me in church. The first thing he asked was if I had heard about the bear. When I replied, "Yes," he showed pictures of it on his cell phone. He had a game camera in his backyard where he put a molasses-soaked salt block for deer. The black bear had been caught on camera in multiple photos as it nonchalantly ate the entire salt block. It was a big, healthy bear, perhaps three hundred pounds. Viewing the pictures, I was dumbstruck with the reality of bears close by. I told Judge Whitley that I was eager to write about the Stanley Creek bear but afraid that any publicity would endanger it. He agreed.

Two days later, Whitley emailed me not to worry any longer about maintaining silence about the black bear. A local Stanley woman, Sydney Szymanski, had seen a big, healthy bear in Harper Park, near Stanley Creek, and shot video of it with her phone. She called WBTV News, and they featured the Stanley Creek bear on television and online. According to Szymanski, when the bear spotted her, it immediately turned and walked away. Seeing the bear scared Szymanski, and she warned others in the park to beware. The Stanley Creek bear was becoming famous. Or was it several bears?

With knowledge of the Stanley Creek bear now common and widespread, I decided to write this essay. As part of my research, I googled "Bears Stanley NC" and "Bears Mt. Holly NC" to see if there were other recent sightings. The internet produced two more local stories about black bear encounters. The first involved a confirmed sighting of a mother with her cub near Mt. Holly on June 21, 2017. The second was a bear that "came out of the woods of Stanley-Lucia Road" on August 7, 2017. The latter was caught on camera close to Stanley Creek. This was almost certainly the same bear (or one of the several bears) reported by others near the Stanley Creek Forest, captured in photos by Judge Whitley's wildlife camera, and seen by Ms.

Szymanski in Harper Park. If this was a transient bear, it had stayed in the forest for more than a month. The sighting of the mother and cub earlier this summer was even more hopeful because it suggested the possibility of a local breeding population.

Back at church on October 22, 2017, Judge Whitley gave me more information on bears around Stanley and connected me with his source, McKinley Puckett, whose family operates Puckett Brothers Autos in Stanley. Calling Puckett the next day brought more local bear news. Over the last month, several customers had showed him pictures that he felt confident were at least three different bears. In September, a hunter in a deer stand snapped pictures of a black bear eating from a corn pile off Airport Road extension, near the Mariposa Road and NC Hwy 27. The next week, pictures were taken of a bear in a field near the Alexis Volunteer Fire Department just north of Stanley. Puckett thinks these were the same bear. But pictures of a black bear standing and eating at a bird feeder on the Black Snake Road are of a magnificent, larger animal. In addition, Puckett saw pictures of a black bear near the intersection of Old NC Hwy 27 and Stanley-Lucia Hwy that looked different from the others. He also recounted that a mother bear and cub were seen near Springfield Elementary School near the intersection of Hickory Grove Road and the Stanley-Dallas Highway this summer. Puckett believes there will soon be a good breeding population of black bears if locals do not shoot them. But he wonders whether folks can resist the destructive urge to kill.

The Stanley Creek bears are trailblazers on the leading edge of a surging mountain population. More will follow. The habitat is just too rich and wild not to attract others pushing further east and looking for living space. With restraint from local hunters, the newcomers will raise cubs and establish a viable population. The big, unanswered question remains whether local folks will accept these majestic, wild creatures or instead eliminate them out of fear or bloodlust.

I myself have still not spotted a bear in the Stanley Creek Forest, although my friend, auto-repair shop owner Stephen Farmer, saw one leave my property to cross Willowside Drive near the Stanley Creek Bridge. With so many eyewitness encounters, the presence of bears is no longer a matter of speculation. Less than fifteen miles from downtown Charlotte, there are several very real black bears on Stanley Creek—not poetic phantoms.

After more than a 200-year exile, bruins ramble through the woods, rewilding and restoring part of the Stanley Creek Forest's older nature. For all who love the natural world in all its fullness, this is a cause for celebration and a sign of hope. As we face unprecedented threats to creation and life itself from climate change, deforestation, pollution, and species extinction, an even greater lesson may be that human ingenuity and science-based interventions (in this case wildlife management), used unselfishly, retain the capacity to restore parts of creation. The black bears on Stanley Creek are living proof.

Index

INDEX